CHANGE YOUR THINKING
#
CHANGE YOUR WORLD

Proven Techniques For Finding Happiness and Meaning in Your Life

Written by *Tess Howells*

IBIS
PRESS

Published in Australia by

IBIS PRESS
Post Office, Narrawong, Victoria, Australia 3285
www.thrivepositivepsychology.com

National Library of Australia Cataloguing-in-Publication entry

Creator:	Howells, Tess, author.
Title:	Change your thinking, change your world: proven techniques for finding happiness and meaning in your life / Tess Howells.
ISBN:	978-0-9946055-1-1 (paperback)
Notes:	Includes bibliographical references
Subjects:	Change (Psychology)
	Happiness.
	Self-help techniques.
	Self-realization.
	Self-actualization (Psychology)

Dewey Number: 158.1

Copyright © Tess Howells 2014

All rights reserved. Other than for the purposes and subject to the conditions prescribed under the Copyright Act, no part of this publication may be reproduced, stored in a retrieval system, or transmitted in any form or by any means, electronic, mechanical, photocopying, recording or otherwise, without the prior permission of the publisher.

First published 2014, reprinted April 2015, June 2016

Text design by Jock Allan
Cover design by John Healy
Printed by OMNE Publishing
www.omne.com.au
24123

Thoth - the Egyptian Ibis-headed God of knowledge and wisdom; the patron saint of scribes and of the written word.

DEDICATION

To my parents Pam and Tom Howells for teaching me resilience and that all people are born equal.

To my children Niki, Tom and Keira for enriching my life.

To Nigel for your unconditional love, support, and encouragement.

ACKNOWLEDGEMENTS

There are so many people who have assisted in the process of this book coming together. First and foremost this work would not exist without the contributions of the many, many clients I have had the privilege of working with over the years. Thankyou for trusting me with your stories and allowing me to walk alongside you for a while.

I am blessed to have a wonderfully supportive family – my parents, my siblings, my children. You always see my strengths and potentials, even when they are obscured from me. A special thankyou to my sister Pam and my brother-in-law Tony, who nurtured me through some of the bad times and helped me to celebrate the good times (usually with a great meal and a bottle of Coonawarra red).

To my dear friend Annie Lanyan, a gifted writer and editor, who has supported and encouraged my writing in the way that only a true friend can – with great sensitivity, but also a directness and honesty that was invaluable. Thanks also to Mary-anne Maylor for an enduring and valued friendship.

Thankyou to Jock Allan and John Healy and OpenBook Howden for offering me the chance to get this work out of my clinics and into the broader public domain. And many thanks to my wonderful and very patient personal assistant, Jacqui Holmes, who provided me with so much support quietly behind the scenes.

And finally, to my friend Cate Allan, who travelled life's ups and downs with me for many years before passing away in 2007. I know you would be happy to see this book come to light. I miss you.

CONTENTS

Preface 1

A Night in the Forest – One Person's Experience of Depression 5

The Paradox of Our Age.. 9

Chapter 1 – Why Are So Many So Unhappy? 11
    Breakdown of Community 15
    Breakdown of Family and Changing Gender Roles 15
    Decline of Religion. 16
    Lack of Perceived Safety and Trust 17
    Changes in Environment– Increased Toxicity, Soil and Mineral Depletion 18
    Technological Change and Overwhelming Levels of Information About All That is Going Wrong! 19
    Loss of Values. 19

Chapter 2 - What Does the Research Tell us About Happiness? 23
    Why Pursue Happiness?. 31

Chapter 3 – What Science Tells Us About Our Brains and 'Reality'.. 33
    Quantum Mechanics. 33
    Epigenetics 34
    Brain Plasticity 35

Chapter 4 – Know What You Can Change and What You Cannot 43
    You Cannot Change Anyone Else 43
    You Cannot Change the Past 46
    You Can Change Your Thoughts 49
    You Can Change Your Emotions 52

Chapter 5 – Proven Strategies for Dealing with Difficult Emotions. 57
    The Fight or Flight Reflex 59
    Calming The Fight or Flight Reflex – B-M-T 60
    Abdominal Breathing Technique. 64
    Cognitive-behavioural Therapy (CBT). 64
    Thought-Field Therapy (TFT), Emotional Freedom Technique (EFT), Tapping 67

    Mindfulness and Acceptance and Commitment Therapy (ACT). . . .71
    Reaching for a Better Thought or Feeling 75
Chapter 6 - Focus Attention on What You DO Want, Not on What You DON'T Want 79
    My Ideal World. 82
    State an Intention 83
    Use Visual Cues 83
    Affirmations 84
    Gratitude 86
    Meditation 87
Chapter 7 – Tell a Different Story 91
    Narrative Therapy 91
    Women's Stories Vignettes. 94
Chapter 8 – The Importance of Values.. 101
    My Primary Values. 109
Chapter 9 – Identify Your Character Strengths 113
    The Future I Am Creating. 115
Chapter 10 – Set Intentions and Goals.. 117
    Goal Setting and Motivation 121
Chapter 11 – Maintain a Healthy Mind and Body 123
    The Industrialisation of Our Food 123
    Why is This Happening?. 127
    Integrative Medicine. 131
    Omega-3:Omega-6 Imbalance 131
    The Brain-Gut Axis 133
    How Healthy is Our Health System?. 135
    What Can We Do to Ensure Good Nutrition for Ourselves, Our Families and Future Generations? 140
    The Principles. 141
    Top Mood Boosting Foods 145
    The Importance of Exercise. 145
    My Health and Wellbeing Inventory. 147

Chapter 12 – Invest in Positive Relationships 149
    Spheres or Bubbles of Perception. 150
    The Importance of Communication for All Relationships. 151
    Listening For Understanding 154
    Reflective Listening 156
    A Word About Introverts Versus Extroverts 158
    Nurturing Your Positive Relationships. 159
    An Inventory of My Current Primary Relationships 163

Chapter 13 – Nurture Your Soul 165
    Spiritual Connection to the Earth 166
    Secular Spirituality. 169
    The Importance of Ritual and Ceremony 173
    Ways to Enhance Your Soul Connection 176

Chapter 14 – Get Involved in Life.. 177

Epilogue. 185

List of Illustrations 187

Graphs and Tables 187

Recommended Reading and Sources 188

Preface

My clinical practice overfloweth with sad, lost, confused, lonely people – and their children. I have been booked out usually six weeks in advance for the past few years and I'm getting tired!! There has to be a better way to help people to help themselves. I think that over the years we have become far too dependent on 'the experts' to tell us how to live our lives – personal trainers to manage our physical health; personal and professional coaches to help us achieve our goals and succeed in our career; nutritionists and dieticians telling us what to eat and what not to eat; consultants of all descriptions helping us to make decisions about how to decorate our homes or how to pre-pay and plan our funerals; and of course psychologists and psychotherapists to help us manage our emotions, our children, our pasts, our futures.

Why have we surrendered control of our lives to people who barely know us? Have we lost faith in our own ability to know what is good or right for us? Why do the statistics suggest we are getting depressed and anxious in record numbers? Have we stopped trusting our own intuition, judgement and inner guidance?

I want to write something that will help you get back in to the driver's seat of your own lives – heading in the direction *you* want to head – hopefully a different direction to the therapist's office! I want you to get back to trusting that you all have unique knowledge, talents, skills, strengths and aptitudes to live your lives in meaningful, purposeful ways and that *YOU are the experts on YOU*.

How? I want you to get to know yourself again – or perhaps for the first time.

Writing this gives me a sense of déjà vu as I recall that as a young woman of twenty I felt lost, sad and disconnected whilst I was travelling overseas in London.

I reported in an earlier book I wrote called *Get Up and Go Up* that I visited a small library at that time in Middlesex and came across a little book called *Be Your Own Best Friend*. It was a small, tatty book – and I was embarrassed by its title and about being seen reading it - so I tried to hide myself in a corner of the library while I read this little book cover to cover. It was the first time in my life that I had been confronted by the question 'Do I like myself?' – I had never considered that before and the question made me feel uncomfortable. Did I even know myself? That little book started me on a journey of self-discovery that I can't imagine will ever end.

As I said earlier, it seems that we have handed responsibility over to others to define who we are, how we should be, what we should do, how we should feel and behave, and often the advice of various "experts" conflicts and overwhelms us. Is it any wonder that we sometimes feel confused, inadequate, anxious and disconnected – from ourselves and others?

But the good news is – that you already have all you need to live a self-directed, meaningful, happy, prosperous life, you always have, you've just forgotten and become disconnected from that knowledge of yourself.

This book aims to take you through a series of exercises that are designed to help you *re-member* all that you are and all that you can be. (*Re-membering* is a term from Narrative Therapy, which is intended to suggest the notion of putting parts of yourself back together – reconstructing the person you choose to be. Narrative therapy is discussed more in Chapter 7.)

I have read prolifically about the emerging fields of neuroscience and neurogenesis, epigenetics, positive psychology and emotional intelligence; about quantum physics, philosophy, nutritional and environmental medicine, Buddhism and spirituality and the factors that contribute to our wellbeing and happiness.

Hopefully I have succeeded in condensing much of what I have learnt into this book in a format that is easy to understand, with exercises and activities that are designed to assist you to rediscover what matters and how you can start living more authentically and completely. The vast majority of these exercises have been scientifically validated through rigorous research by pre-eminent researchers in their fields and have been developed and tested over the years through clinical trials. I too have had the opportunity to test these various theories and their applied strategies within my clinical work as I have assisted my clients in their journey from depression to emotional freedom and happiness.

Although scientific rigour is important, it is not the be-all and end-all. Much has been completely re-written in recent years, about the brain for example, as our knowledge has increased due to quantum physics and technological innovations such as MRI scans, which allow us to 'see' inside the brain. What we thought we knew fifty years ago has been found to be completely wrong. As far as I know, science has not yet validated the existence of God, but that doesn't stop millions of people around the world (including many scientists)

Preface

from having a deep connection with God, or the Universe, or a higher power. The field of energy medicine, is an example of an exciting and promising new paradigm in Western medicine (though it has been used for centuries in the East). It is gaining in popularity and respect as our understanding that all matter within our universe is energy continues to grow through the science of quantum physics. Much of the demand for innovative, alternative or complementary medicine has been consumer-driven, as many find the ten minute medical consult to diagnose and then treat with drugs unsatisfactory. Consumers are increasingly interested in holistic or integrated responses to their health concerns: an approach that acknowledges the interconnectedness of mind, body and spirit.

I have used cutting-edge techniques with my clients in clinic. Some techniques have been scientifically validated, some have not, but they have always been holistic and have often achieved dramatic and unexpected success. I have never subscribed to one particular psychological theory, or treatment protocol.

Rather, when I work with my clients in clinic, I work eclectically, utilising a kit-bag of techniques which is in the room with me, and I tentatively toss out to the client whatever technique that I feel intuitively may be a good fit for them, for the issue, for the time, and I invite the client to engage (or not) with it. If it doesn't work well, we try another technique.

I have never undervalued the role of 'gut-feeling' or 'intuition' that either I or my client may experience throughout our clinical work together and I will often encourage further investigation of these feelings. I have been trained and educated in many psychological therapies, but I am not attached to any one in particular. As a therapist, I prefer to 'fly by the seat of my pants', go wherever the client may lead us, drawing on a broad range of proven and emerging techniques. In this way I have witnessed profound, significant and lasting change for my once troubled clients. This book aims to share some of what is in my kit-bag (or dilly bag as my Aboriginal friends would say), with you and I invite you to try the techniques and use whatever feels helpful.

I feel privileged to have witnessed many clients' re-engagement with the essence of themselves and the empowerment that comes from living their lives with confidence and purpose from a position of self-knowledge, self-acceptance and connection to others. I know this is possible for you – but you will need to take your time in this busy world of ours. Stop, be still, be present, be open – and you may be amazed by the transformation that takes place.

Tess Howells - Psychologist

A Night in the Forest – One Person's Experience of Depression

My feet are pounding the gravel road with such determination that audible expulsions of air are forced from my lungs. Breathing in seems difficult, and at times small, squeaky, child-like whimpers slip out of my mouth into the cool May air. I feel too exhausted to cry. I don't want to experience another thought or feeling – ever. I am tired of the pain, tired of life's disappointments, tired by my own resilience. Get up, get knocked down; get up, get knocked down; get up, get knocked down. Enough is enough – no more. I am a loser – I have failed in my marriage, failed in my business, failed my children by making such poor choices. They will be better off without me. I am a miserable, pathetic, waste of space.

The gravel road gives way to the moist forest floor and my thudding feet carry me deeper and deeper into the forest. I must get as deep into the forest as I can. I will be safe there. No-one will be able to reach me. No more let-downs, no more struggles, no more demands, no more pain – finally. Leave me alone! I walk furiously, turning and weaving through the trees, deliberately leaving the main tracks, desperate for complete isolation and emptiness. No-one will find me here – no-one can get to me.

I start to notice the tall eucalypts, the dense damp brush – I smell the forest scents and at times hear a wallaby jumping nearby. Funny, I think, I don't feel afraid, even though it is starting to get dark. I had always wanted to go alone into the wilderness when I lived in Tasmania, but my fears had stopped me. I was afraid of noises in the dark, of animals taking me by surprise, I was afraid of losing my way. I feel a surreal calmness, as if the forest is my protector. I never want to leave. I am in my own private world – I think about all those other people 'out there' in the other world, being busy doing all those things people have to do, just as I did before today. I want no part of it. 'Ha-ha', I laugh, 'they don't know I am here. He-he, no-one can get to me'. I feel strangely euphoric. (Am I going mad?)

After nearly three hours of walking I was deep, deep within the forest. I lay down on the moist, leaf-dense floor and felt a serenity that had been lacking in my life for years. I was raised outside religion and the closest thing I had ever had to a spiritual experience was a sense that something may exist that was beyond my capacity to imagine or understand. This had happened on only a few occasions, usually out in nature somewhere, when gazing at the vast night sky. But this night in the forest, I felt another presence; I did not feel alone. Is this what people experience as 'God'? It was a clear, cool, starry night and the moon was almost full. 'I am ready to go', I thought. 'I feel perfectly relaxed about it – I have tired of this world and I am ready to go to the next, if there is one'. It all felt so natural, so peaceful, so comforting. I loved it there, hidden away in the forest; I smiled as I embraced my complete solitude and revelled in the idea that no-one knew I was there. I imagined I would just fall asleep and pass into the next world at some stage during the night as the temperature dropped. Beautiful! Perfect! I settled in to my leafy, mossy bed, completely at peace about never seeing another sunrise, not having to survive another torturous day. Ahh – the peace, the tranquillity – such a long time since I had felt these emotions, or was it the absence of negative emotions that gave me such comfort? Bliss.

Suddenly, those feelings were shattered. I remembered my youngest daughter would be waiting for me outside her place of work (her after-school job). I saw her beautiful, innocent and confused face wondering why I hadn't come. 'I am the closest person in the world to her.' She had already lost her father – she would be devastated by losing me too. 'I have to get out of here and go pick her up!'

I knew I was miles into the forest. I had no idea where I was, nor if I could find my way out. It had taken me about four hours to get myself lost. This forest covers an area of 3,000 hectares and over the years a number of walkers have gone missing, never to be found.

And yet, as I got to my feet and started walking, I felt happy, serene and confident that I would be guided out of the forest, if that was what was intended for me.

It's the strangest thing, but now I was walking with a spring in my step; I was smiling, and conversing with 'God' about how wonderful everything was. All of my senses were acute, yet I felt no fear. The fragrance of the eucalypts glistening in the moonlight, the star-filled night sky that I would sing about as a child, the cool wind gently whirring through the trees and bushes – all comforted me, reminding me of happier times. I hadn't been deserted.

I walked and walked for hours, and felt that I was going round and round. On a couple of occasions I came to boundary fences and heard cows – I walked around the fencing, wishing I had learnt to navigate by the moon and stars. At last I saw a line of electricity pylons and became excited thinking that I was just east of where I lived. I was wrong and that unsettled me. I knew I had to keep walking. I was beginning to tire when I came to a main highway. I walked along it looking for a property where I could ask for help to get my bearings. I was confused – I couldn't recognise things. I crossed a bridge over my local river, but it didn't look right to me. Perhaps things are distorted in the dark? After another thirty minutes or so of walking, I saw a farm house with lights on. I knocked on the door. A woman answered and I told a story about having become lost in the forest and that I needed to ring my sister, so she could come for me and collect my daughter from work. I sensed that the woman knew that something was wrong, despite my brave face. I had come out of the forest at the complete opposite end to the point where I had entered – a distance of approximately 25 km. Since I had been walking around and around deep within the forest for much of the time, I must have walked over 30 kms that night. My legs and hip joints ached for days afterward.

I would not describe myself as a religious person. There is still a lot about organised religion that troubles me. Yet that night was full of experiences that defy explanation. I had walked into the forest that afternoon in unbearable pain, desperately seeking relief.

Somehow, whilst I became deeply lost within the forest, my soul found a way out – and my despair was transformed to hope; my disconnection to connection; the ugliness of the world replaced by beauty once more.

"Comfort" – ink drawing by Annette Taylor

The Paradox of Our Age

We have bigger houses but smaller families;
more conveniences, but less time;
We have more degrees, but less sense;
more knowledge, but less judgement;
more experts, but more problems;
more medicines, but less healthiness;
We've been all the way to the moon and back,
But have trouble crossing the street to meet the new neighbour.
We built more computers to hold more information to produce
more copies than ever,
But have less communication;
We have become long on quantity,
But short on quality.
These are times of fast foods but slow digestion;
Tall man but short character;
Steep profits but shallow relationships.
It's a time when there is much in the window, but nothing in the
room.

- His Holiness the 14th Dalai Lama

Chapter 1 – Why Are So Many So Unhappy?

I am more and more convinced that our happiness or our unhappiness depends far more on the way we meet the events of life than on the nature of those events themselves.

Wilhelm von Humboldt

In spite of increasing wealth and longer lives, statistics suggest that we in the Western world are much unhappier now than we ever have been in previous times in history. We have higher levels of depression and higher levels of chronic illness and more crime than fifty years ago. Although we are living longer, we are not necessarily living better.

The World Health Organisation has identified Major Depression as the fourth leading cause of disease burden in the world in 1990 and estimates that by 2020 it will be the second highest cause of disability behind cardio-vascular disease.[1] In the United States 25% of people will suffer at least once in their lifetime from some form of mental illness; 30,000 commit suicide each year and the risk of depression in young people today is three times the rate it was ten years ago.[2] In my clinic over recent years I have seen increasing numbers of young people - primary school and high school age - with severely disabling symptoms of anxiety and depression, including sleep disturbance, self-harming, alcohol abuse and risky sexual behaviours and an increased number of children referred for assessment for autism, attention-deficit-hyperactivity-disorder, eating disorders and conduct disorders. 'Going to see my psychologist' – has sadly become as routine for many young people as going to take a bath.

The most recent Australian data (ABS, Causes of Death, 2009) reports six deaths by suicide each day, or one every four hours – however this is believed to be under-reported. Australian men are four times more likely to die by suicide than women; indigenous Australians four times more likely to die by suicide than non-indigenous and there are higher rates of suicide in our country areas compared to the cities.

According to the World Health Organisation, depression is the most costly disease in the world; on average, treating a single case of depression costs about $5,000 per year, and there are around ten million cases annually in America.[3] In Australia, depression-related disability is estimated to cost the

Australian economy $14.9 billion each year with treatment costs estimated at $600 million annually.

This huge cost to the Australian economy is in spite of the fact that fewer than 50 per cent of those reporting symptoms of depression actually seek treatment and of those who do, those treated with medication do not always show improvement. The research shows there is little benefit in treating those with mild and moderate levels of depression with anti-depressant medication, although this often remains the treatment of choice by medical practitioners. 'Selective serotonin reuptake inhibitor (SSRI) treatment produces a 50-percent improvement in only about half of those who maintain therapy, while about 30 per cent of depressed patients discontinue medications before six-weeks are complete.'[4] 'For very severe depression....the drugs showed reliable effects, but for moderate or mild depression, the effects were non-existent.'[5]

The financial costs to the Australian community however are only one part of the story. As a psychologist, not only am I directly involved in assisting young people and adults now being referred for the treatment of mental health issues, but I am also involved in assisting individuals and communities in the recovery and healing process following suicide.

It is heartbreaking to witness how many lives are impacted within a rural community by the suicidal death of one of its own, particularly the sense of guilt many feel for personally failing the deceased – a view that is so common and so difficult to move on from. Health professionals are members of the community too and are similarly impacted by these events experiencing many of the same difficult emotions.

The incidence of anxiety disorders has also risen and now affect 1.3 million adult Australians annually, with onset being reported generally in early to late adolescence.

Various research studies report anxiety disorder prevalence rates between 5.7% to 15.4% in children ranging in age from 7 to 11 years old, and rates of 8.7% to 17.7% in adolescents aged 12 to 18 years old.[6]

Chronic illness such as diabetes, heart disease, and obesity has exploded, as has childhood disorders such as autism (rates have more than doubled in Australia in the six years from 2003 to 2009[7]), asthma and attention-deficit hyperactivity disorder, whilst at the same time, the quality of our air, water, soils and foods has declined significantly.

Changes in Rates of Selected Reported Chronic Diseases, 1980-1994				
(per 100,000 members of the US population)				
Disease	1980	1994	% Change	Mineral deficiencies Associated with Disease
Heart Conditions	75.40	89.47	+18.67	Chromium, Copper, Magnesium, Potassium, Selenium
Chronic Bronchitis	36.10	56.30	+55.98	Copper, Iodine, Iron, Magnesium, Selenium, Zinc
Asthma	31.20	58.48	+87.44	Magnesium
Bone Deformities	84.90	124.70	+46.96	Magnesium, Calcium, Copper, Fluoride

Source: USDC, 1996, Werbach, 1993. Nutrition Security Institute - www.nutritionsecurity.org

A whole range of services and products has emerged to allegedly help us with our depression and unhappiness, including medications produced by the multi-billion dollar pharmaceutical companies. The internet is full of self-proclaimed experts offering information on how to solve our problems – but we often don't even know what their credentials are. It is not uncommon for a new patient to start our first session by telling me what their diagnosis is because they have already self-diagnosed after reading information about their symptoms on the internet. There is so much information available to us these days through various forms of technology, but although we have an abundance of *information*, we seem to have a dearth of *informed judgement, understanding* and *wisdom*.

I read a post on my Facebook page recently that said 'An informed person knows that a tomato is a fruit, but a wise person doesn't put tomato in a fruit salad.'

It can be difficult for people, and especially young people, to apply the information they receive so easily within a values-based or ethical context, that allows them to make appropriately informed and wise decisions. One example of this, which I have become aware of through my clinical work, is that many young men are 'learning' about sexual relationships with women through watching pornography on the internet. Many have come to the conclusion that women enjoy anal sex as well as giving oral sex and having intercourse in a variety of positions. Recent research in the United Kingdom has shown that the vast majority of 14 to 15 year olds have seen pornography, which has included anal sex and bestiality. Young boys mostly say they enjoy looking at the sites and are repulsed by pubic hair; whilst many of the girls say they are confused, angry and frightened and confirm that boys expect to have porno-sex in real life. Dr Valerie Voon of Cambridge University has conducted clinical trials confirming changes to the reward centre of the brain in young men who regularly view pornography. The reward or pleasure centre of the brain is a collection of brain structures together with the neurotransmitter dopamine, which when stimulated, for example by eating food or having sex, delivers pleasurable sensations and focuses our attention so that the stimuli are repeated.

Repeating behaviours such as eating and having sex is clearly important to ensure our survival, but the reward or pleasure centre is also involved in creating and maintaining addictions, for example, to drugs and alcohol, or as in Dr Voon's study, to the viewing of pornography. In clinic, I have seen not only young men with pornography addiction, but mature and happily married men, whose addictions have had devastating effects on their spouses, their family relationships and their employment.

I have also counselled young men concerned about the size of their penis, because it was not as big as those of the men on those same pornography sites. (Incidentally, the latest research conducted by Indiana University confirms previous studies that the mean size of a human erect penis is 14.15 cm or 5.57 inches).[8]

In previous eras, whether you consider it a good thing or not, we were guided by members of our extended families, our elders, religious or civic leaders, who were respected within our communities, but these days families are breaking down, communities are fragmenting and religious or spiritual connection has become irrelevant to many. Whether one agreed with or accepted the prevailing moral and social codes, they were at least clear and one could take action to either live their lives in accordance with them, or take action to reduce their impact or change them. By contrast, in current times where civic, community, religious or secular values seem either lacking or confusing, I believe many people feel uncertain in their roles, beliefs and expectations and that this contributes to anxiety. A common response to this anxiety and social disconnection is to seek quick fixes through rampant consumerism, mind-altering drugs and substances and short-lived individualistic pleasure-seeking. Relentless exposure to advertising that targets children, adolescents and adults encourages us to distract ourselves from our unhappiness by buying the latest products that promise the perfect figure, the perfect partner, the perfect job, the perfect complexion and unimaginable ecstasy.

Clearly, the statistics relating to the Western world's incidence of depression and anxiety tells us that these approaches are not working.

We seem to have lost control over several areas of our life and now more than ever are over-informed, over-managed, over-socialised, over-medicated, over-analysed, over-worked, over-fed, over-shopped and OVER IT!

What has happened in a generation to produce such unhappiness and lack of physical and emotional health? What is different about our lives in the 21st Century compared to fifty years ago?

Well, the last fifty to eighty years has seen significant social and environmental change, much of which can be attributed to unprecedented advances in science, technology and medicine, but what has this rapid change done to our social institutions and our health and wellbeing?

Breakdown of Community

People are much more mobile now than in previous times, relocating for work and changing employment several times throughout their working life. This is particularly true in rural Australia, where the majority of young people leave the towns of their birth to seek work or attend further education in the cities, but often do not return. People are engaged in less voluntary or community work, attend church and sporting events less and watch more television. Research shows that on average people spend around 25 hours (per week) watching television and this viewing time takes our available hours away from other pursuits. Since most of us are working more, these hours tend to come from social time.[9] All of these factors lead to a lack of continuity within communities and a chance for citizens to develop ongoing relationships of mutual trust and respect with peers and civic leaders.

Breakdown of Family and Changing Gender Roles

In the 1960s the contraceptive pill gave women greater control over their fertility and their choices about whether to have children, and when and how many children to have.

This gave women the opportunity to consider a greater role in the paid workforce and during the 1970s and 1980s there were many social reforms to facilitate this including part-time work, maternity leave, and access to quality and affordable child care. Women's increasing economic independence, along with reforms in family law including no-fault or consensual divorce, lead to women leaving unhappy, controlling or abusive marriages, which they might previously have endured for the sake of their children. With more women participating in the workforce (about two thirds of women with children have some form of paid work outside the home), children are often spending more time in care; both men and women are involved in domestic labour and child-rearing, though women still do considerably more than their male partners, contributing to the stress and fatigue of many women I see as clients. Many families with children report feeling stressed by juggling the responsibilities of caring for their children and their homes with the responsibilities of their work.

Currently divorce rates in Australia are approaching one in two, with the average length of a marriage being around ten years. Divorce rates for remarriages are higher still and the rate of divorce amongst remarriages involving children is seventy per cent.[10] Almost half of all Australian children now live in a home where one of the adults is not their biological parent, with many of them moving from one household to another on a weekly or fortnightly basis, often from a very early age.[11]

Up to fifteen per cent of children are reported to be suffering from a diagnosed anxiety disorder[12] with many children saying they feel anxious about something bad happening to one of their parents. Access to information through various technologies has provided children with graphic images of hurricanes, tsunamis, earthquakes, violent political clashes and more. I have seen many children in my clinic who are afraid to go to sleep, because they fear one of these natural disasters or conflicts might happen to them.

Women who used to be carers and volunteers at our schools, hospitals, health and community services are now in the paid workforce and often simultaneously caring for their own elderly parents or disabled children.

Decline of Religion

In 1901, in Australia's first census year following federation, 96.1% of the population identified as Christian; 1.4% as other religions; and 0.4% as no religion. In 2011, the most recent census, 61.1% identified as Christian; 7.2% other religions, with considerable growth in Buddhism; and 22.3% (nearly one in four) Australians identified as 'no religion.'[13] Traditionally, religious leaders and religious doctrine has provided its citizens with moral guidelines, rules for 'good' living, but religious morals cannot, nor should they, take the place of secular ethical values, particularly in a society of diverse religious view and significant change. Part of the decline in religion in the Western world is precisely because many view the Church's moral position on contemporary issues such as gender equality, contraception, and sexual preference as out of step with community values. As reported by Hugh Mackay in his book *Right or Wrong*: 'Instead of being the province of paternalistic religious leaders, the power to make enlightened moral choices now passes to each individual, each family and each community. Liberated from the yoke of religious prescription, morality can quite properly be seen as a secular pursuit: we are not going to be 'good' because our religious beliefs demands it of us, or because our faith points to rewards in heaven, but because we want to work out a way of living that allows us to be at peace with ourselves and each other.'[14] In fact, more than being at peace with ourselves and others, our personal happiness, as we shall see from the research in Chapter Two, is very much linked to our values and beliefs, but how are we to formulate and give expression to these?

Lack of Perceived Safety and Trust

In recent times, crime rates have risen, and crimes are reported more graphically and regularly via television, print media and increasingly social media. Who can forget the relentless screening of the destruction of the twin towers in New York in 2001? Nightly our televised news services graphically report on wars, famines, earthquakes, mass shootings and all manner of human and natural disasters and are broadcast at an hour when many children are still up and watching TV with their family. Is it any wonder that many of us, especially our children, feel unsafe and that that lack of safety manifests in anxiety disorders?

In response to the question: "Would you say that most people can be trusted – or would you say that you can't be too careful in dealing with people?"

> In 1959:
> 56% of Britons and Americans said YES, most people can be trusted,
>
> but by 1998: those answering Yes had fallen to
> 30% of Britons and 33% Americans (in the mid 1960s)[15]

The percentage of Americans saying that people lead "as good lives – moral and honest – as they used to" was more than half (51%) in 1952, but by 1998 had dropped to only 27%.[16]

The lack of integrity and honesty that has been emerging from various corporations, governments, churches creates an environment where it is difficult for the consumer or citizen to trust those who are in a position of exerting power over them. For example, the extent of the sexual abuse of children by clergy; the greed and manipulation of those involved in perpetuating the global financial crisis; the deceit of food producers in chemically altering our food; our governments attempting to keep secrets from its citizens in relation to the surveillance of private information and the extent to which some forms of industry pollute – all of these things undermine our sense of security and safety and have us living in fear of what might happen next and feeling powerless to change anything.

Changes in Environment– Increased Toxicity, Soil and Mineral Depletion
In the Western world, there have been significant changes in our food supply over the past fifty years. We use more herbicides and pesticides in agriculture and animal management and we chemically alter much of the food that we eat.

There is a widespread lack of adequate nutrition in the agricultural soils in which food is grown and in the food harvested from it. There is a critical need to address the alarming loss of topsoil, fifty per cent of which has been destroyed in the last fifty years as a result of the overuse of inorganic fertilisers, erosion and unsustainable farming practices, which deplete the soil of essential nutrients. Depleted soils cannot grow healthy, nutrient rich food for animals, nor for humans. The nutrients in the food we eat are essential for all our body's biochemical processes.

Nutrient deficient soils grow nutrient deficient crops, which are unable to defend themselves against attack from pests and fungus – which is responded to by modern-day agri-business by spraying more pesticides, thereby continuing the cycle of destruction and pollution.

Without the essential minerals, trace elements and vitamins needed by our bodies to maintain good health, together with the exposure by ingestion and air-borne pollution, more and more people will develop chronic diseases as outlined in the table, *Changes in Rates of Selected Reported Chronic Diseases, 1980-1994.*

Another dimension to the changes in our natural environment and our air, water and food quality are that these are all more things that cause us to be anxious – anxious about obesity, about getting cancer, about the future for our children and grandchildren.

Sadly, I have seen far too many young women with hideous, debilitating eating disorders, which completely robbed them of any positive self-regard and positive emotion and caused their families considerable distress; I have counselled young children fearful about eating the wrong foods and about becoming fat and I remember seeing a woman who was so anxious about what was happening to the earth's environment that she was in a constant state of hypervigilance that seriously impacted on her relationship with her husband and child as well as her own health. This poor woman could not watch television, could not listen to radio, could not read newspapers, could no longer enjoy working outside in her garden and avoided contact with other people in order to avoid exposure to any negative information about the state of the environment. Increasing numbers of children and adults are experiencing anxiety about global warming and how it may impact our lives with increasing extremes in weather and increased susceptibility to droughts, floods and bushfires.

Technological Change and Overwhelming Levels of Information About All That is Going Wrong!

The widespread introduction of technology has seen unprecedented levels of restructuring in our economy as manufacturing industries either collapse or respond to technological innovation. The nature of work has changed with access to personal computers, the internet and digital data transfer, with many workers now able to do their jobs from any location. We have become part of the global community in conducting business and trade, which has improved our access to new markets, but increased our vulnerability to economic downturn in the economies of our trading partners.

Our social relationships are increasingly conducted through technology with an explosion of social media sites including Facebook, Twitter, etc. with a whole new short-hand language developing to enable faster, shorter communications.

World news is updated frequently – we can become overwhelmed with the sheer volume of updates on our televisions and social media sites, the emails that come in to our personal computers at home – and much of this news is negative – reporting on disasters and tragedies – leaving many of us feeling frightened and helpless.

Loss of Values

The political and social landscape has changed much over the last fifty years, and we need a new paradigm where the individual citizen is encouraged to be much more involved in determining the values and principles of living a 'good life' that are appropriate for *them*, but that are also beneficial to the wider community – a concept often referred to as 'the common good'. Martin Seligman, the founder of Positive Psychology, calls the post-war move towards individualism and consumerism and away from community and ethics a 'Waxing of the Self and a Waning of the Common' and says:

> *'The life committed to nothing larger than itself is a meagre life indeed. Human beings require a context of meaning and hope.*
>
> *We used to have ample context, and when we encountered failure, we could pause and take rest in our setting – our spiritual furniture – and revive our sense of who we were.   I call the larger setting the commons. It consists of*

a belief in nation, in God, in one's family, or in a purpose that transcends our lives.[17]

Interestingly, many of the people I see who are depressed or suicidal often care very much about integrity, ethics, and meaning and have felt alienated by a world that seems to reflect little of these values back to them, including the greed of the corporate world and the dehumanising of the medical or health system, which primarily continues to focus on pathology, its biological causes and the prescription of drugs.

When I ask a client when they attend for their first therapy session, 'What would you like to achieve from attending these counselling sessions?', ninety-nine per cent say, 'I just want to be happy', but when I ask them, 'In what ways would your life need to be different in order for you to be happy?' they often don't know. Many of my clients will simply tell me that there is something missing in their lives – there is no sense of meaning or purpose for them in the day to day busy-ness that they are routinely engaged in.

What is it that is missing for so many of us? What is it that the very cerebral world of science, money, technology, and information is failing to deliver to increasing numbers of us?

Personally, I believe it is a spirituality, a concern with the interior landscape – and that is not the same as religion. 'Spirituality I take to be concerned with those qualities of the human spirit – such as love and compassion, patience, tolerance, forgiveness, contentment, a sense of responsibility, a sense of harmony – which bring happiness to self and others. ...There is thus no reason why the individual should not develop (these inner qualities), even to a high degree, without recourse to any religious or metaphysical belief system.'[18] To me, the Dalai Lama is describing a secular spirituality, or what I would call 'an ethical life', or a 'life lived well.'

My clients often talk about their sense of alienation and disconnection, a lack of belonging, a lack of meaning, a lack of guidance and support in how to live their lives well, or worse, cynicism about whether it even matters. As one of my favourite writers, Thomas Moore, says in the opening lines of his book *Care of the Soul*: 'The great malady of the twentieth century, implicated in all of our troubles and affecting us individually and socially, is "loss of soul". When soul is neglected, it doesn't just go away; it appears symptomatically in obsessions, addictions, violence, and loss of meaning. Our temptation is to isolate these symptoms or to try to eradicate them one by one; but the root problem is that we have lost our wisdom about the soul, even our interest in it.'[19]

As a psychologist, I found Thomas Moore's reframing of depression as 'sickness of the soul' very liberating and helpful. Rather than seeing the symptoms of depression, including retreat from the outside world, the disconnection from others, and the withdrawal inwards, as pathology (which medical practitioners would rush to 'fix' with anti-depressants), he believed that such withdrawal was in fact essential in order to be able to hear the desperate voice of soul trying to communicate what was needed for emotional and spiritual health. Once I began to engage with my clients in conversations about 'soulfulness' or their sense of 'spirituality' in their lives, encouraging them to transcend the immediate, day-to-day challenges, there was a richness and hopefulness in those narratives that had previously been lacking.

Whilst we have professionals to advise us on how to live just about every dimension of our life, we have no soul advisers – or advisers to assist us to remember and reconnect to our soul and perhaps we should be grateful for that, since we can avoid having our 'soul' corrupted by the outside interference of others. I have been told that Indigenous communities have traditionally referred to the symptoms of depression as 'soul sickness', which in the contemporary Australian context has become manifest in alcoholism, obesity and diabetes, violence, family breakdown and disconnection. Through my clinical work with Aboriginal health centres, I have talked (or yarned, as they would say) with many Aborigines, who feel cut adrift in a world that cannot acknowledge, let alone, encourage and support a sense of identity that is intimately connected to the land, to ancestors, to the animals and plants through dreams and visions and dreaming stories and songlines. How is Western medicine to heal their soul sickness without narratives that elucidate and validate these things? We are not speaking the same language.

I have come to believe that Soul reveals itself through a self-determined balance of attachment and connection to others on the one hand, with the solitude of the interior life on the other – reflection, contemplation, acceptance of all that it is to be human.

Even the former scientific researcher Martin Seligman, who described himself as: '(having) wavered between the comfortable certainty of atheism and the gnawing doubts of agnosticism my entire life…'[20] began to think that there was 'something more'. 'I feel, for the very first time, the intimations of something vastly larger than I am or that human beings are. I have intimations of a God that those of us who are long on evidence and short on revelation (and long on hope and short on faith) can believe in.'[21]

In framing a new response for psychology to the challenges of the twenty-first century, I think we can no longer ignore the place of soul or spirituality in the process of assisting our clients regain or perhaps gain for the first time a wholeness that embraces all that is possible for human endeavour.

That being the case, how do we go about getting more soulfulness, connection, meaning and purpose in to our lives?

(Endnotes)

1. Murray & Lopez (1996) *Global Burden of Disease Study*; Mathers & Vos cited in Mental Health Research Institute, Depression Awareness Research Project (Melbourne: 2003) p.36
2. Stefan Klein PhD, *The Science of Happiness: How Our Brains Make Us Happy – and What We Can Do To Get Happier* (Aust: Scribe, 2006) p. xvii
3. Seligman, M. Flourish – *A Visionary New Understanding of Happiness and Wellbeing* (Aust: Random House, 2011.)
4. Logan, A.C. "Neurobehavioural Aspects of Omega-3 Fatty Acids: Possible Mechanisms and Therapeutic Value in Major Depression". *Alternative Medicine Review*, Vol 8, Number 4, (2003).
5. Seligman, M. Flourish – *A Visionary New Understanding of Happiness and Wellbeing* (Aust: Random House, 2011)
6. "What is Anxiety?" Anxiety Recovery Centre Victoria. Accessed July, 2013. http://arcvic.org.au
7. "Autism in Australia, 2009" Australian Bureau of Statistics – Accessed July, 2013. http://www.abs.gov.au
8. Herbenick, D. "Erect Penile Length and Circumference of 1,661 Sexually Active Men in the United States". *Journal of Sexual Medicine*. Accessed August, 2013. http://onlinelibrary.wiley.com
9. Layard R. *Happiness – Lessons from a New Science*. (UK: Penguin, 2006).
10. Australian Institute of Family Studies
11. Australian Institute of Family Studies
12. "What is Anxiety?" Anxiety Recovery Centre Victoria. Accessed July, 2013. http://arcvic.org.au
13. "Major Religious Affiliations 1901-2011", The Australian Collaboration, Accessed July, 2013. http://www.australiancollaboration.com.au
14. Mackay, H. *Right and Wrong – How to decide for Yourself*. (Aust: Hodder, 2004).
15. Layard, R. *Happiness – Lessons From a New Science*. (UK: Penguin, 2006).
16. Layard, R. Happiness – *Lessons From a New Science* (UK: Penguin, 2006).
17. Seligman, M. *Authentic Happiness*. (Aust: Random House, 2002).
18. Dalai Lama. *Ethics for The New Millennium*. (USA: Riverhead, 1999).
19. Moore, T. *Care of the Soul – A Guide for Cultivating Depth and Sacredness in Everyday Life*. (USA:HarperCollins, 1992).
20. Seligman, M. E. P. *Authentic Happiness*. (Aust: Random House, 2002).
21. Seligman, M. E. P. *Authentic Happiness*. (Aust: Random House, 2002).

Chapter 2 - What Does the Research Tell us About Happiness?

There has been an explosion in recent times of what I call 'happiology' – a plethora of discourses and resources about how to be happy. Some of these seem to be useful, but I find many to be mindless and self-indulgent and just a new substitute for the reverence for consumerism.

When I talk about happiness in this book, I am not referring to the shallow and individualistic pursuit of pleasure. I am referring to a more sustainable and meaningful sense of physical and emotional wellbeing, which benefits individuals and communities. This distinction is important to me for several reasons. Firstly, I am interested in teaching people how they can live *overall* more happy and meaningful lives, not just have more pleasurable experiences some of the time. Secondly, I believe that our own happiness or wellbeing is intimately linked to the welfare of others around us – we are social beings and we affect and are affected by others. I will say more about this in the chapter on 'What the Research Tells Us About Our Brains.' Thirdly, I want my readers to have confidence that what I am asking them to do will work for them, because it has been thoroughly researched and tested. I have read widely in the field of happiness and have studied eminent researchers in the field of the science of happiness including Martin Seligman, Richard Layard, The Dalai Lama, Daniel Goleman, Daniel Gilbert, Tal Ben-Shahar, Stefan Klein, Matthieu Ricard, and Richard Davidson, among others. Finally, I have noticed that there is a growing tendency to label everything concerned with happiness as 'positive psychology' as though the terms are interchangeable and I think this does a great dis-service to the researchers I have mentioned and is a complete misunderstanding of the science of Positive Psychology.

The Positive Psychology movement has been borne of the experiences of many eminent traditional psychologists, who at the turn of the new millennium were increasingly dissatisfied with the poor results that had come from traditional psychology's focus on problems and difficulties with life.

It was a movement located within a socio-political context of change and hope for a new future, at a time when the Western world was experiencing unprecedented high levels of depression, anxiety and general dissatisfaction with life, in spite of increasing prosperity. It was also a time when many were questioning what the basis of a 'good life' was following the failure of the economic rationalists to deliver one; when rampant consumerism and individualistic self-interest had not delivered us from the mass malaise; when the loss of community, church and spirituality were just starting to be noticed and mourned; when the over-pathologising and medicalization of our social ills led to many disengaging altogether from social and political life, bombed out on either prescribed or illicit drugs. Not much has changed in the decade since.

It was within this socio-political context at the start of the 21st century that Martin Seligman began to seriously question traditional psychology's achievements over the previous four decades. Seligman was an esteemed professor of traditional psychology at the time, who had spent years working at the "rats and stats" end of the profession, was an academic who was well published and highly regarded by his peers, and had been elected to be President of the American Psychological Society. He had, however, become increasingly motivated by his own discomfort with the social-political landscape at the time and the poor outcomes for his clients and so he began to wonder about the factors that could lead us to living a more enriched life. A natural pessimist, his greatest motivation came from his then six year old daughter Nikki, who called him a grouch. In his words 'I had spent fifty years enduring mostly wet weather in my soul, and the last ten years as a walking nimbus cloud in a household radiant with sunshine.'[1] From that time on, Seligman decided to switch his research focus away from the factors that make us psychologically unwell towards the factors that would have us flourish and give our lives meaning.

Seligman's very first task was to create a classification and measurement system for human strengths and virtues - as opposed to the Diagnostic and Statistical Manual (DSM) – the existing classification system for mental disorders.

Seligman assembled a team of researchers at the University of Pennsylvania who spent years reading, analysing and classifying all the major religious and philosophical texts throughout history in order to find ubiquitous human virtues that could lead us to live a good life. As Seligman reports, "Led by Katherine Dahlsgaard, we read Aristotle and Plato, Aquinas and Augustine, the Old Testament and the Talmud, Confucius, Buddha, Lao-Tze, Bushido (the Samurai code), the Koran, Benjamin Franklin, and the Upanishads – some two hundred virtue catalogues in all. To our surprise, almost every single one of these traditions flung across three thousand years and the entire face of the earth endorsed six virtues:

Seligman's Six Core Virtues and Character Strengths:

1. **Wisdom and Knowledge**
    - Curiosity/Interest in the World
    - Love of Learning
    - Judgement/Critical Thinking/Open-Mindedness
    - Ingenuity/Originality/Practical Intelligence/Street Smarts
    - Social Intelligence/Personal Intelligence/Emotional Intelligence
    - Perspective
2. **Courage**
    - Valour and Bravery
    - Perseverence/Industry/Diligence
    - Integrity/Honesty/Genuineness
3. **Love and Humanity**
    - Kindness and Generosity
    - Loving and Allowing Oneself to be Loved
4. **Justice**
    - Citizenship/Duty/Teamwork/Loyalty
    - Fairness and Equity
    - Leadership
5. **Temperance**
    - Self-control
    - Prudence/Discretion/Caution
    - Humility and Modesty
6. **Spirituality and Transcendence**
    - Appreciation of Beauty and Excellence
    - Gratitude
    - Hope/Optimism/Future-Mindedness
    - Spirituality/Sense of Purpose/Faith/Religiousness
    - Forgiveness and Mercy
    - Playfulness and Humour
    - Zest/Passion/Enthusiasm[2]

Seligman argues that taken together the Virtues encapsulate the notion of 'good character'. He goes on to classify each of the virtues into Strengths of

Character, twenty-four in all, as outlined above. He argues that once we know what our key strengths are, we need to make sure that we have the opportunity to give them expression through our daily activities and this will lead us to experience authentic happiness.[1*]

So, Positive Psychology emerged from rigorous research and has always rooted its definition of 'happiness' in something so much more than the individualistic pursuit of hedonistic pleasure. It has always been concerned with notions of 'good character', virtue, ethics, all of which acknowledge our relationships with others and concern for the 'common good.'

Martin Seligman has gone on to revise and develop his theory, as all good researchers will and now talks about 'flourishing' and 'wellbeing' rather than happiness, partly because of the overuse and lack of meaning of the word.

Seligman says in his latest book *Flourish*:

> *'I actually detest the word happiness, which is so overused that it has become almost meaningless. It is an unworkable term for science, or for any practical goal such as education, therapy, public policy, or just changing your personal life.'*

He goes on, perhaps in response to those who have mistakenly lumped positive psychology in with happiology:

> *'[T]he modern ear immediately hears 'happy' to mean buoyant mood, merriment, good cheer, and smiling. Just as annoying, the title (Authentic Happiness) saddled me with that awful smiley face whenever positive psychology made the news. 'Happiness' historically is not closely tied to such hedonics – feeling cheerful or merry is a far cry from what Thomas Jefferson declared that we have the right to pursue – and it is an even further cry from my intentions for a positive psychology.'*[3]

It has also often been wrongly reported in the media that positive psychology rejects and discourages people from accepting their so-called negative emotions and places unrealistic expectations on people to be happy at all times. This simply is not the case. Positive psychologists encourage their clients to accept and embrace the full range of human emotions. Indeed, it is often the 'negative' emotions (I don't think any emotion is negative; they all serve a purpose) such as anger, sadness and disappointment that offer us contrast to the more positive emotions of happiness, contentedness, joy, etc.

---

1. * You can take the test to identify your strengths at www.authentichappiness.org and click on *VIA Signature Strengths Survey*, or it is included in Seligman's book *Authentic Happiness*.

How is one to fully appreciate love or happiness for example, if one has no experience of loss, emptiness, sadness or pain? It is the very *contrast* of our emotions that provides the richness of our lives and the desire to live our lives well. It is entirely appropriate that one would feel sadness, distress, even depression following the loss of a loved one or a relationship breakdown; it is a normal response to feel anger if you feel you have been treated unjustly.

Positive psychologists want to teach people the skills to pass through these emotions rather than become stuck in them and Positive Psychology has learnt from the research that there are things we can do to move ourselves from unhappiness to wellbeing and that for sustainable happiness we need to have more in our lives than simply good mood.

Seligman had developed his theory from *Authentic Happiness* based on self-reported measures of life satisfaction. He found, however, that these would change depending on how the respondent felt at the time of being questioned, so he moved to a five element definition of Wellbeing instead.

Five elements of Wellbeing Theory (PERMA)

1. Positive Emotion;

Subjective experience of pleasure

2. Engagement;

Being fully immersed in a task or activity, "flow"

3. Positive Relationships;

The contribution of others to our lives

4. Meaning

Belonging to and serving something that you believe is bigger than the self

5. Accomplishment

Success, mastery or achievement for its own sake

Other researchers in the science of happiness field, including Ed Diener, Professor of Psychology at the University of Illinois, and in more recent times his son Robert Biswas-Diener, have also conducted extensive and robust research around the globe in an attempt to unravel the factors that contribute to happiness. Their research, not dissimilar to Seligman's, found that there is an optimal level of happiness in which people do not seek euphoria, but pursue life satisfaction, meaning, and frequent positive emotions, with recognition that some negative emotions are an integral part of a happy life.[4] They refer to this more sustainable type of happiness as 'Psychological Wealth', which consists of the following essential components:

Psychological Wealth – Essential Components:
• Life satisfaction and happiness
• Spirituality and meaning in life
• Positive attitudes and emotions
• Loving social relationships
• Engaging activities and work
• Values and life goals to achieve them
• Physical and mental health
• Material sufficiency to meet our needs

You will no doubt notice immediately the overlap between the results of the global research of the Deiners and the research results of Seligman and his team.

In his book *Happiness – Lessons from a New Science*, Richard Layard, a leading economist and Member of the House of Lords, reports on U.S. research that identified 'The Big Seven Factors' affecting happiness:

The Big Seven Factors (Affecting Happiness)
• Family Relationships
• Financial Situation
• Work
• Community and Friends
• Health
• Personal Freedom
• Personal Values

I think it is probably already clear from the work of the above primary researchers in the field of happiness research that there is significant convergence of the findings conducted across the globe around what it is that we need to pursue to make us happiest in the full context of that word. That is very useful, because this convergence or agreement allows us to design appropriate treatment protocols and engage with our clients in a way that will actually make a positive difference.

You may be surprised to learn from the summary of the research that money is less important than many would think, in fact, once you have enough money to meet your basic needs, additional money does not add to your overall level of happiness, as shown in the graph below.

When asked to rate a response to the statement *You are satisfied with your life* on a 7-point scale, ranging from complete disagreement at 1 to complete agreement at 7, where 4 is neutral, there was no difference in satisfaction between the top three hundred richest Americans and average Pennsylvania Amish or Inughuit (Inuit) people of northern Greenland:

LIFE SATISFACTION FOR VARIOUS GROUPS Diener and Seligman, 2004.	
Forbes Magazine's richest Americans	5.8
Pennsylvania Amish	5.8
Inughuit of Northern Greenland	5.8
African Masai	5.7
Swedish probability sample	5.6
International College Student sample (47 nations in 2000)	4.9
Illinois Amish	4.9
Calcutta slum dwellers	4.6
Fresno, California, homeless	2.9
Calcutta pavement dwellers (homeless)	2.9

So, in spite of the efforts of capitalism and consumerism, at the end of the day, it is not accumulated 'stuff' that gives our lives meaning. I have never heard of anyone on their death bed saying: 'Would you mind just getting my Royal Albert vase for me – I want to look at it one more time.' It is nearly always the state of personal relationships that comes into focus and the research consensus is that positive relationships are a much more reliable predictor of happiness.

Key researchers in the field of the science of happiness all acknowledge the existence and importance of the full range of human emotions – those called the positive and negative emotions. All share a definition of happiness which is much broader than personal and fleeting pleasure; a definition that is about a life well-lived within a social context; a life with purpose and meaning; a life that is ethical.

Likewise, Buddhist philosophy, from which much of today's mindfulness therapies have evolved, (see Chapter 5 for more information on mindfulness) acknowledges what the Buddhists call the 'mental afflictions' – states of mind that lead to agitation and a lack of peace. Buddhists practice overcoming these afflictions through mind training focussing on antidotes to the afflictions. For example, for the mental affliction of judgement, one should focus on practising compassion. For conceit, humility. For aversion, acceptance.

So, as with the Buddhists, the Positive Psychologists are interested in assisting people to reduce the severity and impact of their negative emotions – what the Buddhists would call the afflictions – in order to have less suffering. That's less suffering, not NO suffering. Positive Psychologists acknowledge that living is full of challenges, disappointments, losses and suffering. They do not seek to deny, discount, or distract their clients from these necessary and appropriate feelings, as has been claimed in recent times, but rather to assist them to move productively through them.

Whether you call it mind training or mindfulness or something else, this engagement with one's full range of emotions, and the desire to move through negative emotional states, rather than becoming stuck within them, is not just good the for individuals, but for society. It seems the pursuit of our own happiness and wellbeing is as important for our own psychological health, as for the mental health of others. Recent advances in neuroscience have discovered that not only do our emotions affect us; they also directly affect those around us, as we will learn in the next chapter.

In summary, the Positive Psychology movement differs from the happiology movement in fundamental ways.

In my view it is unashamedly political - concerned with getting people reconnected to values, to ethical, purposeful and meaningful living. It is a social revolution seeking to mobilise citizens back to community, to living a 'good life'.

Some countries have now begun to think about the wellbeing of their citizens in a new way, replacing or adding to economic measurements like GDP – Gross Domestic Product – with a concept called GDH – Gross Domestic Happiness, to monitor social and psychological wellbeing. Since 1971 the tiny Buddhist country of Bhutan has rejected the GDP as a measurement of its progress and instead measured its prosperity through Gross National Happiness (GNH) based on the physical, social, environmental and spiritual wellbeing of its citizens. In 2011, following the collapse of much of the western world's financial system, growing economic inequality and environmental destruction, Bhutan called upon the countries of the United Nations to adopt a more holistic approach to development.

Sixty-eight countries endorsed the approach and a UN panel is now investigating ways in which Bhutan's GNH model can be applied around the globe.

Bhutan's Minister of Education, Thakur Singh Powdyel, says 'People always ask how can you possibly have a nation of happy people? But this is missing the point. GNH is an aspiration, a set of guiding principles through which we are navigating our path towards a sustainable and equitable society. We believe the world needs to do the same before it is too late.'[5] Environmental sustainability is a cornerstone of Bhutan's GNH policy leading to government commitments to remain carbon neutral and to ensure that at least sixty percent of the country's total land mass remains permanently forested.

The education system has likewise been adapted to include GNH policies and ensures that all children are taught cultural and environmental practices as well as maths and science. Meditative practice and preparation towards becoming good citizens are essential components of educational policy.

Similarly, here in Australia, Martin Seligman has been very actively involved in recent years in delivering an integrated Positive Psychology programme across the curriculum to all students at the Geelong Grammar School in the state of Victoria – an incredibly exciting project that will teach Australian children values and how to give expression to them from an early age, thereby improving their contribution as good citizens, their wellbeing and reducing the incidence of mental illness in the coming years.

Over the many years that I have practised psychology I have seen countless theories come and go. Many new theories are old theories in new words and whilst most offer some contribution to reducing suffering and enhancing wellbeing, nothing has excited me like Positive Psychology. I believe it is a genuine social and political movement, which has the ability to empower people by putting them back at the centre of their own lives. It can reduce their reliance and dependence on professionals, help them re-engage with their values and civic duties and develop a sense of meaning and purpose that doesn't just enhance their own lives, but enriches the lives of all others around them.

Why Pursue Happiness?

The research confirms that happy people feel healthier, have better relationships, work harder and more productively, make others feel happier, give to others more. So the world is a better place, with fewer problems when more people are happy. Therefore, the pursuit of happiness, or wellbeing is

NOT selfish, quite the contrary, personal happiness enriches self, others and community.

> Happiness resides not in posessions, and not in gold, happiness dwells in the soul.
>
> *Democritus*

(Endnotes)
1. Seligman, M. E. P. *Authentic Happiness*, (Aust: Random House, 2002).
2. Seligman, M. E. P. *Authentic Happiness*, (Aust: Random House, 2002).
3. Seligman, M. *Flourish – A Visionary New Understanding of Happiness and Well-being.* (Aust: Random House, 2011).
4. Diener, E & Biswas-Diener, R. *Happiness – Unlocking the Mysteries of Psychological Wealth.* (USA: Blackwell, 2008).
5. Annie Kelly, The Observer, 2 Dec 2012 *Gross National happiness in Butan: the big idea from a tiny state that could change the world.* http://www.thegardian.com August, 2013

Chapter 3 – What Science Tells Us About Our Brains and 'Reality'.

We are shaped by our thoughts; we become what we think. Buddha

---

Quantum Mechanics

In the last fifty years three emerging fields of science have completely changed our understanding of both our external and internal worlds. Firstly, the field of quantum physics has refuted all we have previously understood from Newtonian principles about the world of matter and now scientists believe that everything in our universe is reducible to energy; that there is no matter, that all things appearing as solid matter (including us) are in fact vibrating energy. Fred Wolfe, an American Quantum physicist says: 'Everything you know about the universe and its laws is more than likely to be 99.99 per cent wrong.'[1] The Quantum Theory has been described as the most successful theory ever discovered and its laws have been proven in every experiment, even though it seems to contradict much of what we thought we knew. In the world of quantum mechanics, atoms are ruled by probability not certainty – a concept that Albert Einstein found very difficult to accept, calling the theory of entanglement 'spooky action at a distance'. Entanglement theory states that measuring one particle affects another, even over considerable distance. Quantum physics has found that there are multiple realities and dimensions and that the perception of reality is affected by the measurer and the place of measuring. The universe is mostly empty; the Unified Field, as it is called, is a field of infinite potentiality; of abstract consciousness and that intention is correlated with outcomes – intention causes materialising. Quantum mechanics asserts that we and everything in the field are ONE.

Does this very complicated field of science have any relevance for us in our pursuit of happiness? Yes. Quantum theory argues that at each moment of your life you can impact this field of energy and influence your reality by your consciousness – every intention, every thought and every feeling has a vibrational match to vibrational frequencies of energy.

Some feelings and thoughts (such as sadness, anger, discouragement) vibrate at a lower frequency and will tend to attract anything that happens to be vibrating at the same frequency. Other feelings such as joy, happiness, peacefulness vibrate at a higher frequency and will attract things to you of a similar nature.

Perhaps you have had some experience of this. I know I have. There have been times in my life when I have felt sad, low in energy, angry about losses in my life, and it has seemed that I just kept getting even more bad luck. It is a common belief that bad luck comes in threes and that is often the reality for many of us. Similarly, I have known others who always seem to attract good luck – often winning money or awards more frequently than most others. Can you recall the feelings of being in love? When people are in love they are vibrating at a very high frequency and it seems as though everything in their lives goes well for them. Their health is good, they enjoy their work and relationships; their self esteem and energy levels are high.

In this new understanding, the power of our own thoughts and feelings is limitless. We can actively use this knowledge to change our vibrational match by monitoring our thoughts and feelings and doing what we can to maintain high frequency vibrations. We will talk about this more in chapters to come. If this is something you are interested to explore more, however, I highly recommend the books written by Esther and Jerry Hicks that are included as recommended reading at the end of the book.

Epigenetics
The second field of science, which has radically altered our understanding of ourselves and our environment is the field of epigenetics. Epigenetics (epi – meaning above) literally means above genetics and refers to switches on top of our DNA that give expression to genes without changing them. The epigene, sitting on top of the gene, is marked to either turn on or turn off the gene. It was only in 2000 that scientists finally identified the human genome and our genetic code was unlocked – or was it? Although scientists were aware of the epigenome, they really didn't understand much about how it influenced genetic expression through generations.

Although epigenetic changes are biological responses to environmental stressors such as diet, stress, and prenatal nutrition, they can be inherited through several generations via epigenetic markers. If the environmental stressor is removed, the epigenetic markers will eventually extinguish and the DNA code will revert to its original programming.

In one fascinating study, Moshe Szyf of McGill University, Montreal, found an epigenetic link between a person's experience of child abuse and suicide risk. 'Child abuse is an environmental factor that leaves an epigenetic mark on the brain. In a comparison of suicide victims who were abused or not, only the abused victims had an epigenetic tag on the GR gene. Interestingly the GR gene receives a similar epigenetic tag in rat pups who receive low quality care from their mothers.'[2]

The new field of epigenetics and the role of environmental stressors on the genetic expression of health indicators for subsequent generations has helped me to understand and give a new context to the inter-generational impact of the Australian government's forced removal of Aboriginal children from their families. It is clear to me now that the trauma this policy induced in the parents who had children taken away from them is evident in those children and their children. It seems to me highly probable that the trauma of the Stolen Generation continues to be acutely felt and experienced by the generations who have followed them as a result of epigenetic changes that have lead to markers on genes that give expression to addiction, obesity and depression. It is imperative that we do all we can to assist the Aboriginal community to heal from this trauma and return their DNA to its original form in order to have any impact on improving the physical and psychological health outcomes for current and future generations.

So you can see that another reason for living our lives well is that we are likely to pass on the impact of our environmental stressors to our offspring and their offspring. But don't feel defeated if you think you have an epigene for a disease or disorder – medicine is already examining and trialling drugs that turn off expression of negative epigenes and turn on expression of positive genes and it is already known that *behaviour* can influence gene expression too.

More research needs to be conducted in this very new field of science and I have no doubt that the role of our thinking and hence our behaviour will prove to have far-reaching consequences. Stay tuned.

Brain Plasticity

At the same time that quantum physics has impacted our understanding of our universe, in less than twenty years, the third emerging field of neuroscience has led to a complete rewriting of all that we thought we knew about the brain historically and has introduced us to the concept of 'neuroplasticity' and 'neurogenesis'.

It was only in 1998 that neuroscientists discovered that new neurons are continually being generated in the adult brain and that brain circuitry is changed by both external and internal events. Neuroplasticity is our brain's ability to adapt to change and 'neurogenesis' is the ability to produce new cells and connections. We used to think that by the time we were adults we had all the neurons we were ever going to have and that from around age thirty they would start dying off. We now know with access to new technologies like MRI scans, that our brains are capable of developing new cells and new neuronal connections throughout our life span; that functions previously undertaken by injured parts of the brain can be undertaken in different parts of the brain and that both internal and external experiences can change our brains in either positive or negative ways.

The way that brain plasticity works was demonstrated brilliantly in a simple and fascinating experiment, which was conducted at Harvard Medical School by neuroscientist Alvaro Pascual-Leone. Pascual-Leone devised a simple five finger piano exercise and had volunteers practice for two hours over five days playing as fluidly as possible keeping to the metronome's 60 beats per minute. At the end of each day's practice session, the volunteers were hooked up to a device called a transcranial-magnetic-stimulation test or TMS for short, which was used to map how much of the motor cortex of the brain controlled the finger movements for the piano exercises.

After just one week of practice, the scientists found that the stretch of motor cortex devoted to these finger movements had extended to take over surrounding areas. In other words, the brain had rewired itself.

But that was not where the experiment ended. Pascual-Leone had another group of volunteers simply *think about or imagine* playing the piano exercise. They played the simple piece of music completely in their heads, holding their hands still. When the data of the two groups was compared, scientists found that the region of motor cortex had expanded in the brains of those *imagining* they were playing in exactly the same way as those who actually played. It was clear that mere thought could alter the physical structure and function of our brains.

You may have heard of elite athletes practising their performances by visualising it in great detail and that their muscles fire up whilst they are sitting still in a chair in exactly the same way as if they were actually competing.

In another experiment I learnt about as an undergraduate, two groups of school children, who were matched on age, intelligence, and socio-economic status were each given the same test. Group A were told by their teacher that they would find the test easy, whilst Group B were told they might find the test difficult. Group A exceeded the scores of Group B by a significant amount. Their thoughts, or beliefs, or expectations affected the outcome.

The act of imagining changes our brains in the same way as the act of doing. We can all experience this phenomenon ourselves when we imagine sucking on a lemon, for example. Take a look at the lemons in the picture on the next page and imagine their fresh, tangy, lemony scent.

The Power of our Brain

Now, close your eyes for a moment and imagine that you are cutting one of those lemons in half. You can see droplets of juice leak out and its fresh sharp lemony smell seems to fill the room. Now pick up one of the halves of the lemon and bring it up to your mouth and take a big bite into it. The sharp, sour tang of the lemon has your mouth puckering and filling with saliva.

OK, so open your eyes. Did you experience an increase in saliva or a puckering sensation in your mouth when you visualised biting in to the lemon? If so, you know you have the power to change your brain with your thoughts and to change your experience of life.

This is exciting news, because it means that we can exercise a greater degree of control over our thoughts, our emotions and our experiences than we might have believed possible. With the right exercises, we can increase our capacity for ongoing happiness.

Some form of mind training is essential to be able to exercise greater control over our thoughts, our intentions and the feelings that arise in order to attract the things that we really want in our lives. And yet mind training is not something that we in the Western world have placed much store in.

In fact, I suspect that even the term 'mind training' conjures up negative connotations such as 'brain washing'. Yet I know from my work as a clinical hypnotherapist, that the power of suggestion can be remarkable.

Matthieu Ricard, a Buddhist monk who is often called the 'happiest man in the world', notes that 'We spend vast amounts of time and money on our physical health, on anti-aging and beauty, but surprisingly little on our minds – which affects all else.'[3] In 2004 Matthieu was involved in a number of experiments under the leadership of neuroscientist Richard Davidson of the University of Wisconsin-Madison, in which he was wired up and had his brain activity monitored by electroencephalogram (EEG) and functional magnetic resonance imaging (fMRI) whilst meditating on compassion. Buddhist monks devote themselves for many years to developing greater compassion, altruism and inner peace. The idea of monitoring their brain activity had first originated at the Dalai Lama's residence-in-exile in 2000 when a group of leading neuroscientists and psychologists attended the Mind and Life gathering on the subject of 'Destructive Emotions.' The results of the study were groundbreaking. They demonstrated that the left frontal cortex is activated by positive emotion and the right frontal cortex by negative emotion. Even more importantly, the mind can influence the brain to change the degree of activity in either, or both sides. All practitioners of meditation who took part showed increased levels of activity in the left pre-frontal cortex, which swamped activity in the right pre-frontal cortex. But the extreme level of activity in the left pre-frontal cortex of Matthieu's brain had never before been witnessed or reported in the neuroscience literature and hence his title 'The Happiest Man in the World'.

Essentially Richardson had shown that mind-training has the potential to alter brain structure in a way that would increase positive affect or happiness and reduce the experience of negative affect.

A number of researchers since that time have conducted studies in which they teach subjects with no prior experience to meditate. The results are encouraging, showing that depression can be relieved and positive emotion increased after as little as eight hours of meditation training.

Recent studies from the Massachusetts General Hospital have shown that just eight weeks of Mindfulness-Based Stress Reduction (MBSR) training can lead to a thickening in the regions of the brain involved in decision-making, learning, memory and perspective-taking and simultaneously a thinning of areas of the brain that are involved in threat and fear such as the amygdala. The creator of the program, Dr Jon Kabat-Zinn, described the results of a MBSR program delivered to people working in a high-tech, high stress work setting in which a shift occurred from having more right pre-frontal cortex activity to more left pre-frontal cortex activity. He reports:

> Until we did that study, it was thought that the ratio of right to left activity in the PFC was pretty much a fixed trait once you reached adulthood – that you were the way you were; if you were a nervous nelly, you were pretty much going to stay that way, and if you happened to be Ms Relaxation, you stayed that way, too. But in eight weeks we saw that right to left shift in what used to be thought of as a fixed emotional set point.

Kabat-Zinn also reported that the group that undertook the eight week MBSR training also showed significantly improved immune response compared to controls.[4]

So the scientific research shows us that our thoughts create our experiences and that we have the power to change our experiences by choosing what we focus our attention on.

Many of us want to make a difference in the world in some small or maybe not so small way. We use our skills and talents in whatever way we can to make a contribution to relieving suffering and increasing levels of compassion, understanding, love and acceptance. But some of us are not at all sure that we have any particularly useful or special talents that would allow us to make any difference at all. If this is what you think, you are wrong.

Apart from the fact that I believe every one of us has unique talents, knowledge and skills – even if you are not yet able to believe that, or feel connected to that – you can still make a meaningful and positive difference to our world. How? By learning mind control and changing your thoughts – and this is why.

Researchers are extending our knowledge further out from just what is going on inside our own heads and brains and looking at what happens when we interact with others. As Daniel Goleman notes in his book *Social Intelligence*, 'Neuroscience has discovered that our brain's very design makes it *sociable*, inexorably drawn into an intimate brain-to-brain linkup whenever we engage with another person. That neural bridge lets us affect the brain – and so the body – of everyone we interact with, just as they do us.'[5] So our own thoughts, whether positive or negative, will also affect those we are in close proximity to. Wouldn't it be better to share positive emotion rather than negative? Have you ever had the experience of being around someone who completely drains you emotionally after hearing their complaints and negativity? Or alternatively being invigorated by spending time in the company of someone who is positive? 'That link (brain-to-brain) is a double-edged sword: nourishing relationships have a beneficial impact on our health, while toxic ones can act like slow poison in our bodies.'[6] More about relationships in future chapters.

Put simply, whatever you think, you will experience, and as our understanding of the human mind develops with recent advances in neuroscience (outlined earlier) it turns out that we affect what others may experience also. This is significant. Louise Hay is a well-known American author of self-help books. When she first claimed in her book *You Can Heal Your Life* that 'We create our experiences, our reality and everyone in it. When we create peace and harmony and balance in our minds, we will find it in our lives'[7] her work was often criticised for being too New-Agey, non-scientific, and airy-fairy. Some (particularly within the health professions) went so far as to say it was dangerous, but it would now seem that Louise, who was writing in the 1980s, was well ahead of her time. There is now scientific evidence that our thoughts and feelings are indeed linked to our experiences and capable of being transferred to others with whom we engage through recently discovered 'mirror neurons'.[8] Neuroscientists such as Marco Iacoboni have argued that mirror neuron systems in the human brain help us to understand the intentions and actions of other people and are the basis of the human capacity for empathy.

What I find exciting about this is that it gives us all enormous power – not only to influence our own emotions and experiences and therefore the quality of our lives, but to also impact in a positive way the lives of others.

Much of our thinking has become habitual and for many of us that means habitually negative, especially if you are suffering from depression or anxiety. Start monitoring your thoughts and see just how negative your language, evaluations and expectations are. One way of assisting in bringing this to consciousness is to wear an elastic band around your wrist and every time you catch yourself having a negative thought, give yourself a ping. This will really help to bring the extent of your negative thinking in to focus and will help you to catch negative thoughts before they get an emotional hold and cause a spiral downwards in your mood. Then you can use new skills to intervene, disputing the validity of the negative thought and replacing it with a new, less negative or neutral thought.

If we experience negative, worrying thoughts, this will lead to us feeling negative emotions and these emotions are likely to be transferred to those with whom we are in contact.

Similarly, if we experience positive thoughts we will feel positive emotions and these too will be transferred to those around us. This is potentially life-changing and world changing!

The more control we can gain over our thinking, the more we can control how we feel and therefore affect how others feel. Think more positive thoughts and we will feel happier. If we feel happier when we come in to contact with others, *they* will feel happier. If others feel happier, then the overall amount of happiness in the world has grown – and we have contributed directly to that! We have changed the world in some small but significant and positive way.

Change Your Thoughts

⬇

Change Your Feelings

⬇

Change Others' Feelings

⬇

Change the World

In light of the new evidence from quantum physics, epigenetics and neuroscience the pursuit of happiness or wellbeing cannot be considered an indulgent, individualistic or selfish pursuit. Many of my clients (especially women) often think it is, but on the contrary it is a social responsibility, perhaps even a moral duty. We must attend to our own wellbeing and happiness, so that we may in turn impact upon the wellbeing of those around us and steadily increase the overall amount of happiness and wellbeing in the world.

In summary, as with the research into happiness, there is remarkable convergence between the new sciences of quantum physics, epigenetics and neuroplasticity. It shows that we are not in this alone and that we have more power than we imagined to influence our reality. Some social commentators, including the Dalai Lama, have referred to these developments in science as a convergence of science and spirituality:

- Everything in the universe is interconnected; part of a unified whole

- Consciousness affects our perception of reality
- We can change our reality by changing our consciousness (thoughts, feelings, intentions)
- By changing our own thoughts and feelings we impact on the thoughts and feelings of others

So where can we start in this process of change?

(Endnotes)
1. Wolfe, F.
2. http://learn.genetics.utah.edu/content/epigenetics/brain/ 6/9/2013
3. Ricard, M. *Happiness – A Guide to Developing Life's Most Important Skill.* (UK: Atlantic Books, 2007).
4. 30 Maia Szalavitz "Jon Kabat-Zinn Talks About Bringing Mindfulness Meditation to Medicine Health and Family", Jan 11, 2012. http://healthland.time.com
5. Daniel Goleman. *Socal Intelligence: The Revoluntionary New Science of Human Relationships* (New York: Bantam Del, 2006).
6. Ibid
7. Louise Hay, *You Can Heal Your Life* (Aust: Specialist Publications, 1988) p. 7
8. Marco Iacoboni, *Mirroring People: The Science of Empathy and How We Connect with Others* (New York: Picador, 2008).

Chapter 4 – Know What You Can Change and What You Cannot

So the science confirms that we have the power to change our reality, but let's get a little clearer about exactly what we CAN change and what may be beyond our scope of influence. Apart from our ability to have an effect on the emotions of those in proximity to us through mirror neurons, we can never change anyone but ourselves - never, no exceptions.

You Cannot Change Anyone Else
(But you can change how you think about them)

If you have been thinking 'My marriage would be so much better if my husband was more thoughtful', or 'this job would be great if my boss was more encouraging', or 'I wish my sister would stop complaining all the time.' GIVE IT UP! They will not change unless *they* believe that *they need to* and feel compelled to (and in my experience, few do). In any case, what a person may or may not need to do to improve the quality of their lives is essentially none of your business – it is theirs. I have seen this phenomenon so often in my clinical work; the woman who believes her violent husband is going to change and not abuse her ever again; the man who believes his serially-cheating girlfriend will commit to fidelity and never cheat on him again; the mother who believes her drug-addicted son is going to stop stealing from her. So many times whilst working with others in therapy, I have had clients tell me that they stay in toxic relationships in the hope that they can change their partner, in spite of there being no evidence that their partner wishes to change or even has any awareness of the impact of their behaviour on the other party. This belief is erroneous and futile and will only lead to your own exhaustion – and I should know – I stayed in an unhappy marriage for much longer than I should have in the belief that I could make my unhappy husband happier. I have learnt that lesson now – the only happiness that I need to be concerned with is my own and if I take care of that, the rest will take care of itself. Think about it for a moment, if you are spending a vast amount of your time and energy trying to change others, or meet their needs, or make them happy, you are not living YOUR life, you are intruding into theirs.

And when we think we know better about how someone else should be living their lives, we make them wrong. We communicate to them that they are not good enough, and not only are they not good enough, they don't even know how to go about getting to be good enough! Even if we are acting with good intent, it is an arrogance on our part to think we know how another should best live their life and it disempowers the person we claim to be caring about. Our actions can in fact divert them away from their true path. I love this story about the butterfly:

The Story of the Butterfly

A man found a cocoon of a butterfly. One day a small opening appeared. He sat and watched the butterfly for several hours as it struggled to squeeze its body through the tiny hole. Then it stopped as if it couldn't go further.

So the man decided to help the butterfly. He took a pair of scissors and snipped off the remaining bits of cocoon. The butterfly emerged easily, but it had a swollen body and shrivelled wings.

The man continued to watch it, expecting that any minute the wings would enlarge and expand enough to support the body. Neither happened. In fact the butterfly spent the rest of its life crawling around. It was never able to fly.

What the man in his kindness and haste did not understand: The restricting cocoon and the struggle required by the butterfly to get through the opening was a way of forcing the fluid from the body into the wings so that it would be ready for flight once that was achieved.

Sometimes struggles are exactly what we need in our lives. Going through life with no obstacles would cripple us. We will not be as strong as we could have been and we would never fly.....

(Author Unknown)

To be in a satisfying, loving relationship, we need to accept our partner unconditionally. To make our love conditional on our partner changing, puts us in a position of struggle or resistance, which in quantum theory terms, is a position of low frequency vibration, because we are focussing our attention more on what we don't have, or what we don't like, or don't want, rather than on what we *do* want. I am not suggesting that you should tolerate abusive or violent behaviour for example, and we will talk about this more in future chapters, but a relationship that is conditional on meeting our needs and wants is disrespectful to our partner/family member/friend. It is our job to meet our own needs and wants and our happiness is down to us – it is never up to others to make us happy.

Quantum physics tells us that all emotions are vibrating energy providing you with feedback. So called 'negative' emotions such as anger, frustration, sadness, disappointment are telling you that you are not in vibrational alignment with what you want – you are in alignment with what you don't want. So you will need to try to reach for better-feeling emotions that are more in tune with your desires. At the end of this chapter I have included some exercises that are designed to help you diminish the effects of negative emotion and move you towards more positive emotion.

But whilst you cannot change another person, you can always choose to change your feelings *about* that person, or about the behaviours that bother you. I remember, when I was studying clinical or medical hypnosis reading about the problem of snoring being a problem for the snor-ee, that is, the person sleeping with the snorer. The hypnosis treatment was directed to helping the snor-ee to be less bothered by the snoring. Snoring rarely bothers the snorer – except if they are concerned about their partner's disturbance.

Similarly, if we are bothered by something our partner, child, friend, relative is doing, it is really our problem. Often the other party isn't even aware that it is bothering us. We need to change our thoughts and hence our feelings in relation to the irritation if we want the relationship to endure.

EXERCISE:

If you are in a relationship that you want to continue but the other party does things that upset you, your only option is to change your thinking about that person, the behaviours that bother you, and the nature of the relationship.

Try focussing for just one week on all that you find positive about the person and do not give attention to the things that bother you. Give positive feedback about what they do well and choose to suspend all negative criticism. You may be surprised by how your changes can effect changes in your partner.

In subsequent chapters we will be looking in more detail at some techniques that will facilitate this surrendering of resistance and shifting of emotions from low-frequency vibration to higher frequency vibration.

You Cannot Change the Past
(But you can change your thoughts about the past)

We tend to experience negative emotion most when we are focussed on past experiences or negatively predicting future experience. I always tell my clients who have been referred for anxiety disorders that anxiety is generated by negative, worrying or fearful thoughts about the past or the future; that it is difficult to experience anxiety if we are fully focussed on the present moment.

PAST	PRESENT	FUTURE
Memories of negative events	Focussed on sensory imput	Prediction of negative events
Negative emotion	Neutral/positive emotion	Negative emotion

For example, if you are thinking about being alone and wanting a partner in your life and you have the thoughts: 'I never have luck with relationships. I always get hurt.' and you begin to remember past hurts and experiences, visualising them in your mind, maybe even replaying hurtful words or interactions, you will most likely end up feeling a range of negative emotions, some of which may include sadness, anger, disappointment, embarrassment, rejection, fearfulness. Then, you will often move your thinking from the past to the future and have thoughts like 'What's the point of trying to find anyone. It's bound to end in disaster, as usual. All the good ones are taken. I don't want to get hurt again.' Your negative thoughts now both in the past and the future will have you thinking that nothing will change and will leave you feeling powerless, depressed and hopeless.

The truth is that in the course of living our lives things happen. And sometimes bad things happen to good people. That's the stuff of life and sometimes it seems unfair. But the very stuff that seems bad often ends up down the track being exactly what you needed. For example, I have had many challenging and difficult times in my life and at the time I could not make sense of them. Why were these things happening to me? I tried to be a good person, I tried to never do harm to others, but still things went wrong and there were many setbacks and disappointments. Now, however, as a practising psychologist, I am so grateful for all the difficulties that I have experienced and grown from, because I believe they have contributed to making me a better psychologist

– one with capacity not to judge, to empathise easily and to always maintain hope that things can be better.

I have also counselled many clients who made contact at the time of distressing relationship breakdown, only to come across them several years later telling me that they are happier than they have ever been and know now that the relationship they were in was not right for them. Similarly, clients have been distraught about not getting the job that they so desperately wanted at the time, only to find themselves in a new position that ended up being so much better.

If you want to have different, new and positive experiences, then you will need to think different, new and positive thoughts.

You cannot hold onto thoughts that are inconsistent with what you want to achieve. And remember, it doesn't matter as far as your brain is concerned whether you believe it is true or not – it is still important to mentally rehearse it the way you want it to be. If we return to the previous example of feeling lonely and wanting to have someone come in to our lives, we could mentally rehearse these new thoughts: 'I am now attracting a new, caring partner into my life. The past does not predict the future. I am open to meeting someone who really cares about me.' Take time to imagine in great detail what it will be like when you do have the man or woman of your dreams in your life. How does that feel? Mentally rehearse the *feeling* as well as the thought. Visualise regularly, but especially first thing in the morning and last thing at night – because these are the times when our brain waves are naturally slower, and similar to our brain wave pattern when in hypnosis. You can hypnotise yourself by relaxing yourself physically and mentally and then imagining what you want, and how it feels when you have it, in as much detail as you possibly can. Remember from the experiments with the students imagining to play the piano. Their brains rewired in a way that would make playing the piano easier, even though they hadn't even touched a piano!

> **EXERCISE:**
>
> Think about something that you would like to happen in your life.
>
> Write it down in present tense as though it was happening, e.g. 'I now have a wonderful, thoughtful, kind and generous partner who loves me unconditionally.' This is called an **affirmation** and I advise clients to put their affirmations up in a place where they can see them at each end of the day (usually on their bedroom wall).
>
> **Visualisation**: Each morning when you awake, and each night before you go to sleep, repeat your affirmation two or three times, and then try to *feel* what it would feel like if your desire had come true. See this playing out in your mind in as much detail as you can – where are you, what are you doing together, what sensory information is around you (i.e. what can you see, smell, hear, touch, taste?) Really try to *feel* what it is like to be in the relationship of your dreams and believe that this is possible for you.

Esther and Jerry Hicks in writing of the teachings of Abraham[1]* in their book *Ask and It Is Given*, talk about the negative experiences of our lives providing us with contrast – contrast to the positive experiences – and the contrast – the yin and yang of our lives if you like that Chinese concept – helps us to get clarity about what we DO want in our lives, by giving us experiences of what we don't want.

If your attention is on the past – STOP. The Past Does Not Predict the Future. The past is gone and there is nothing that you can do to change whatever happened, but you can change your thoughts about it. If you can find a silver lining in any difficult circumstances in your past, that's great, but if you can't it doesn't matter. It only matters that you don't keep lining up with the low-frequency feelings of what you don't want by thinking and feeling past stuff.

If you find yourself overwhelmed by strong emotions of the past, practise this technique to bring yourself into the present:

---

1. * Abraham is a group of non-physical entities that are "interpreted" by Esther Hicks. For more information about Abraham or Esther and Jerry Hicks refer to their book *Ask and It is Given* (USA, Hay House, 2004)

> **Sensory Focus**
>
> Wherever you are at the time of experiencing overwhelming, or strong emotions, or feeling panic or anxiety, ask the following questions and they will have you firmly back in the present:
>
> **What do I see?** Focus your attention on at least five things that you can see around you. Pay attention to the detail. What colours, textures, shapes?
>
> **What do I hear?** What are the noises that are around you at the moment?
>
> **What can I smell?** Are there any particular scents or fragrances where you are?
>
> **What am I touching, feeling/in contact with?** What is the texture of the things I am in contact with – is it rough or smooth, is it hard or soft?
>
> **What am I tasting?** Is there anything I notice about sensations in my mouth? Are they dry, sweet or bitter?

After paying attention to your sensory experiences in the here-and-now you will find that the symptoms of anxiety will settle and you will be firmly regrounded in the present moment.

You Can Change Your Thoughts

Many of my clients are surprised when I tell them that they have the power to change their thoughts and their feelings. Many believe that thoughts and feelings are somehow automatic – generated in response to external stimuli, but as Viktor Frankl, a survivor of Nazi concentration camps said: 'Between stimulus and response there is a space. In that space is our power to choose our response. In our response lies our growth and our freedom.'[1]

If we can learn to harness the power of the potential in that space, we have the power to relieve ourselves of much of our negative emotion and suffering, as Viktor did when he endured the most horrific and dehumanising experiences, by maintaining control over his thoughts. He had little to eat, lived in a depressing, squalid environment, saw his friends become ill and die but he maintained control over his thoughts and never lost hope.

He said: 'Everything can be taken from a man but one thing: the last of human freedoms – to choose one's attitude in any given set of circumstances, to choose one's own way.'[2] Viktor Frankl's story is remarkable and told in his book *Man's Search for Meaning* and gives so many inspiring examples of how mind control can help us to overcome the most demanding of challenges.

Remember from the chapter on the latest developments in neuroscience: They show us that we have the ability to reprogram our own minds and by doing so we can rewire our brains and develop new neural connections within it. Laying down neural pathways is a little like creating a groove on a record or CD – the more you think a certain thought, the deeper the groove becomes and over time this becomes your default setting.

If you are thinking a negative thought, or a thought that is not serving you, or is not consistent with the goals for your future, you need to actively start laying down a new thought that is more consistent with your desires. Think it regularly, thereby creating a new neural pathway. Over time, the new thought, if continually rehearsed, will form a deep groove, whilst the former negative one will fade and eventually disappear, just like a track through the bush that has not been used for a long while and becomes overgrown and forgotten.

Illustration of neural pathways:

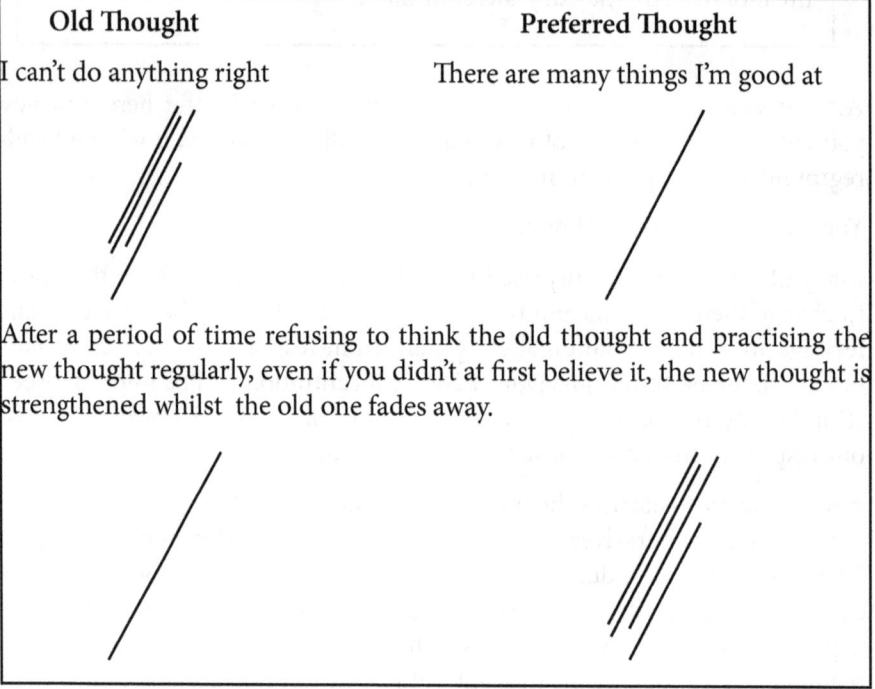

Old Thought	Preferred Thought
I can't do anything right	There are many things I'm good at

After a period of time refusing to think the old thought and practising the new thought regularly, even if you didn't at first believe it, the new thought is strengthened whilst the old one fades away.

Know What You Can Change and What You Cannot

I never used to understand this concept. I have always had what my friends have described as an 'analytical mind'. I always wanted to understand things right from a very early age.

I was one of those irritating two year olds who drove her parents crazy by asking 'but why?' constantly, and I spent many years of my early adult life trying to understand why I did what I did, why I said what I said, why I felt what I felt, why I thought the way I did, why others felt and behaved differently, why the world was how it was, etc., etc. I just couldn't seem to get relief from the constant thinking, analysing and investigating – except in the occasional binge-drinking episode. I would often talk to others in the hope of getting more clarity and understanding by listening to their perspectives about the events of my life: how I survived a bushfire, a life-threatening illness, a trauma involving one of my children. I thought that by sharing these stories I was showing others my openness to hearing their views and opinions on why these things happened. What was it about me that may have contributed somehow to these events and what would I need to change? I also thought I was demonstrating my resilience and my astounding ability to bounce back and never lose hope. I felt confused when what I thought was my positive attitude didn't seem to contribute to any reduction in the regular visitations of disappointment. What I failed to understand at that time was that I was continuing to focus my attention on what *I didn't* want and so I remained a vibrational match for more challenges and traumas. And guess what, I kept getting more of the same.

In psychology, we call this over-thinking 'ruminating' and understand that rumination can lead to anxiety and depression. But now I finally get it; that by spending so much of my time trying to understand why things were not the way I would like them to be in my life, I kept thinking about, talking about and feeling things that were in alignment with exactly what *I didn't* want more of!

The Buddhists call this overthinking "monkey chatter" and they use meditative practice to quieten this inner cacophony and regain peace and harmony.

It concerns me that much of traditional psychology focusses attention on what is wrong in our lives: on our negative cognitions (thoughts) and emotions and many people, particularly in the United States, spend months or even years talking with their therapists about their problems – whereas by contrast positive psychology encourages us to think about what we *do* want, what is right and how we can maintain positive feeling and wellbeing.

You Can Change Your Emotions

Thoughts and emotions are inexorably linked: negative thoughts = negative emotions; neutral thoughts = neutral emotions; positive thoughts = positive emotions. By learning how to change your thinking to be less negative, you will inevitably experience fewer negative and more positive emotions.

First, I want to emphasise again that it is important to embrace the full range of your emotions. There is no such thing as 'bad' emotions. All emotions serve a purpose. We cannot know the joy of happiness without having to know about sadness. We would not have anything to compare with. Abraham calls this emotional feedback 'contrast' and tells us that it is the gap between the feeling of where we are now and and the feeling of where we want to be. The contrast between the two feeling states allows us to get clear about what we really want, and to change our vibrational alignment to match it.

Negative emotions are appropriate in many situations: the loss of a loved one for example, a failed business, or a chronic illness. So it is important not to struggle with these emotions and attempt to deny them. In my experience, struggling and resistance causes far more psychological distress to the person experiencing the negative emotion and to those around them. Positive psychology is not about denying negative affect; it is about not allowing that negative emotion to dominate and interfere with you living your life productively.

There are things we can do to honour our feelings, particularly when they are linked to loved ones. And yet we can also continue to move toward feeling more the way we would prefer to feel.

This is something that I never used to believe. I thought feelings were feelings and there wasn't much you could do to change that. Sometimes I could stay stuck in uncomfortable emotions for days. I also believed that others were responsible for my feelings. If this person hadn't done this, or this person hadn't said that, I wouldn't be feeling negative emotion; or if this person did this or said that, I would be a happier person. But now I understand that NO-ONE IS RESPONSIBLE FOR MY FEELINGS BUT ME. EVER.

Whenever a client begins a sentence: 'He made me feel…..' 'Or they made me feel….' I invite them to say it differently, acknowledging that their feelings are uniquely their own and always within their power to choose and to change. 'I felt……' When we attribute the reason for our feelings to someone else, it disempowers us. The negative feeling may be uncomfortable, but if we acknowledge it as being within our control to change, we can get some relief from it by applying certain techniques, such as Abraham's *Reach For a Better*

Feeling Technique. Several other successful strategies for managing negative thoughts and emotions are outlined at the end of this chapter.

I first started to read about the creative nature of thoughts way back in the 1980s. In those days it was considered hippy, New-Age stuff and I practiced trying to change my negative thoughts and therefore my negative emotions. I can recall a time when I had to pick up my former husband from his place of work and as was often the case, he was running late. As a working mum, my life was also very busy and demanding at this time, so I was sitting in the car getting angrier and angrier, thinking about all the things I still had to get done. Then it occurred to me that he wasn't affected by my anger; it was me, and only me, who was feeling bad. Given a choice, would I choose to feel angry or would I choose to feel something different? Clearly, I would choose something different.

I would choose to feel calm – after all, this was one of those situations that I could do nothing to change; my anger was certainly not going to contribute anything to improving the situation I was in, therefore, I needed to remember:

If You Cannot Change the Situation:

Your only choices are:

1. **Accept it**
2. **Change Your Feelings About the Situation**

As a result of setting an intention to feel calm and accepting that I could not change the situation I started to notice that it was actually a pleasant, sunny day and that I was waiting in a beautiful natural environment full of trees. It was a very serene place compared with the busy city environment I had just rushed out from. After making this intellectual and sensory shift my 'fight or flight' response (I will talk more about this later) started to settle, my heart rate slowed and I began to feel much more relaxed. I even started thinking how nice it was to have the opportunity to sit and relax with nothing else to do – something that was rare in my busy life as a mother of three children and full-time worker. My breathing became slower and deeper, the tension in my body seemed to dissipate.

Within only a matter of minutes, my anger had completely gone and I felt calm and relaxed. Instead of feeling cranky with my partner when he finally arrived, I greeted him warmly. If I had stayed angry, we would have both gone home to the children stressed and irritable. They would have reacted badly to this and so it goes on. Everyone benefitted from me taking control of my mind and emotions. We cannot always control the events that happen to us in our lives. But we *can always control our thoughts* and learn how to switch our thinking to create more positive feelings and experiences for ourselves and those around us.

I have so much admiration for Viktor Frankl. He exemplified this process of thought and emotional control when he refused to be broken by the harsh conditions and treatment he endured in Auschwitz and Dachau. He survived the many indignities, losses and hardships he suffered by maintaining control of his mind, ensuring connection to hope and transcendence.

> Holding on to anger is like drinking poison and expecting the other person to die.
>
> *Buddha*

EXERCISE:

Whenever you notice you are having negative thoughts and/or feelings:

1. Firstly, just notice it. Don't struggle with it. Struggle and resistance just make it stronger.
2. Do you feel any tension in any specific part of your body? Breathe – try counting In-2-3 and breathe in through the nose; then OUT-2-3 and breathe out through the mouth. Check your body for any signs of tension or tightness and relax any muscles that may be tense.
3. Is the thought you are having consistent with what you want in your life, or is it about what you don't want or have? Change it to be consistent with what you do want.
4. What is the feeling that the thought elicits?
5. Do I choose to feel what I am feeling, does it serve me, or would I prefer to feel something different?
6. Notice sensory information around you and pay attention to what you DO want
7. Reframe and think about how it will feel when you DO have what you want

It may not feel like it to you at first, but you are always in control of your own thoughts and emotions and with practice you can take action to change negative emotion to neutral or positive emotion. In so doing you can help those you come into contact with to feel better too. And remember what the research shows us – that you *do* have the power to rewire your own brain.

(Endnotes)
1. Viktor Frankl *Man's Search For Meaning*. (USA: Washington Square Press, 1984).
2. Ibid

Chapter 5 – Proven Strategies for Dealing with Difficult Emotions

I don't want to give my readers the impression that I think you should all be able to implement the strategies in this book and turn your lives around in an instant. I know from my own personal struggles with negative thinking that these things take time and there is often resistance to change in the beginning. I can say quite confidently though, that if you want to feel happier, more at peace, more connected to others or to something bigger, and you diligently work at matching your thoughts to your desires, you *will* move towards those outcomes.

In the meantime, however, we all have to start from exactly where we are now – and for some of you that means starting from a position of feeling depressed, hopeless, anxious, lost, confused or disconnected. I understand that. So, I have included in this chapter a range of strategies for dealing with uncomfortable, or unwanted thoughts and feelings that may be keeping you stuck. Take your time, be gentle with yourself, and never give up. Sometimes when we least expect it, the light is turned on and the darkness fades – somehow we just get it, when before we couldn't. Often we need to move outside of what we normally do in order to be in a position where new perspectives can reach us.

A while ago I was climbing a steep, extinct volcano and after much effort, I reached the top, only to find another volcano directly behind the first. This second volcano had been completely obscured by the first one and was only visible to me once I had reached the pinnacle of the first volcano. Rather than going directly up the steep side as the pathway of the first volcano had done, the pathway to the second volcano looped around and around from the base to the top (see drawing below). Once I was on top of this second volcano, the view from the top was incredible and not a view that could have been seen from the first volcano. In addition, as the path meandered around on the way up, the 360 degree view constantly changed and gave me differing perspectives of the landscape.

The pathway to the top of the first volcano was more direct and so a shorter distance, but it was much more arduous because of the steep incline and I had a limited view of the landscape. I could only see what was to my left and right. Conversely, the pathway to the top of the second volcano was much longer as it wound its way around the mountain, but its gentler gradient made the walk much less physically taxing. In addition, I had a much broader view of the landscape as I circled around the mountain.

This trek seemed to be a great metaphor about life's struggles. When we are trying to climb to the top, if we are going directly from the bottom to the top, we can become overwhelmed. It seems like such a long way and requires such effort. Sometimes we get stuck, thinking we will never get there. We may become completely overwhelmed or demoralised, turn around and go back. It's just too hard. We need to know that it's OK to rest and that we can choose to go *around* instead of straight up; and that as we go around, drawing closer to the top, our perspective changes; new possibilities become evident that were previously obscured from our view and before we know it we reach the top and can see all the views and all the possibilities.

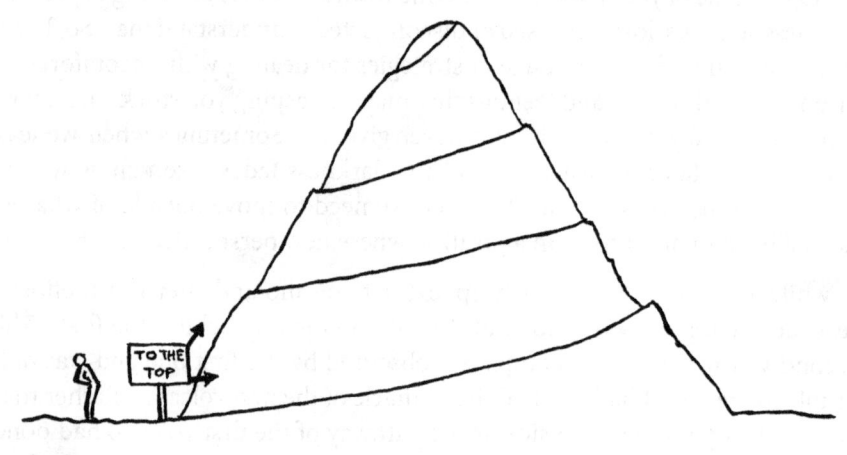

As I mentioned earlier, unlike other writers or therapists, I have no particular connection to any one theory or therapy; or if you like, pathway. I have used all of the strategies included in this chapter at various times with my clients and generally all clients have responded positively to them. However, we are unique individuals and some of these techniques will have more appeal or resonance than others. That's absolutely OK. I really want you to get to know what works for you. Try each of the techniques and then see which ones tend to suit you better and continue to work with those. Find your *own* pathway.

Remember, *you* are the expert on *you*. I am not, nor is any theorist or therapist gone before. But other people's experiences and wisdom can be of assistance as you attempt to navigate your way from unhappiness to wellbeing and a sense of meaning.

The Fight or Flight Reflex

Whenever you are experiencing fear-based symptoms of anger, panic or anxiety you have triggered your 'fight or flight' response. This is a natural reflex that we are all born with. It is designed to protect us from danger. A caveman who came face-to-face with a large predator had two options. He could fight off the attack, or he could run like crazy away from the threatening beast. Whichever option he took, his body needed to prime itself quickly, in order to do more than what was normally required of it. These days, we are not generally confronted by large predators wanting to eat us; our threats tend to be more of an emotional nature. We are stressed by our jobs, financial pressures, responsibilities for children, health concerns. Our fight or flight reflex gets triggered by physical or emotional threats, whether they are real or imagined. Remember from the neuroscience research that our brains respond to imagined stimuli in the same way that they respond to real stimuli. For many anxiety sufferers the fact that the fear is 'irrational' or not real makes little difference to how genuinely frightened or overwhelmed they feel. An explanation of what is happening physiologically may help you understand why.

Whilst in 'fight or flight', also known as arousal of the sympathetic nervous system, a number of changes occur rapidly within our bodies, including:

- Stress hormone including adrenaline is released into our bloodstream to provide energy quickly
- Our hearts beat faster to provide more blood to our muscles to increase our strength
- We breathe more rapidly to increase the level of oxygen in our blood
- Blood-clotting systems are activated to protect against potential injury
- Our muscles tense ready for action
- The process of digestion ceases so that more blood can be directed to the brain and muscles
- Our pupils dilate and our senses become more acute

Once the danger period is over, the calming part of our nervous system, known as the parasympathetic system is activated. Our bodies gradually return to their normal state as the level of stress hormones in our blood diminishes.

Sometimes the 'fight or flight' reflex is referred to as the 'fight, flight, or freeze' response, since a third response to danger is to freeze; to keep completely still and quiet and wait for the threat to pass, much like a frightened rabbit in the headlights of a car.

Calming The Fight or Flight Reflex – B-M-T

When I am working therapeutically to assist a client who is experiencing post-traumatic stress disorder following exposure to a frightening event, I am helping them to find relief from the thoughts and images associated with the initial trauma. Similarly for clients suffering anxiety or panic generated by their fearful thoughts, for example, fear of spiders, or fear of having a serious illness, I am helping them to de-activate their sympathetic nervous system.

One of the easiest and quickest ways I know of getting relief is to practise **B-M-T**, where B stands for **Breathing**; **M** for **Muscles** and **T** for **Thoughts**. I designed this simple technique to deliberately mimic the body's natural response in turning on the parasympathetic nervous system to restore calm following a threat (real or imagined).

One of the positive aspects of the BMT technique is that it can be done anywhere discreetly – no-one needs to know that you are taking yourself through these practices. I have used BMT successfully for many patients, including several of my youngest patients, who have gone on to train their fellow students or their siblings in the practice.

When you are in full fight or flight mode your breathing becomes shallow and rapid. As a result you are taking less oxygen up into your brain and this in turn will trigger the release of stress hormones into your blood stream. Slowing your breath down and increasing oxygen to your brain, communicates that the danger is over and you no longer need the stress hormones.

B = Breathing

Slow your breathing rate down. Breathe in through your nose to the count of 3 – say to yourself IN – 2- 3; hold, then breathe out through your mouth – OUT – 2 – 3. Take at least five breaths. You should notice that your heart beat starts to slow down and you feel some relief from the feelings of panic.

Secondly, take a moment to scan your body and notice where you may be holding tension and just let it go. If you can, sit in a chair and go completely floppy, but if you are driving a car, or you are at your desk at work, you can still relax your muscles without drawing attention to yourself, or compromising your safety. If you are driving, pay particular attention to your shoulder and neck muscles and let go of tension in those areas.

When your muscles are tense, they send through a system of bio-feedback a message to your brain that says 'I need to be ready for some threat' and the brain responds by saying, 'OK – here's some stress hormone for you.'

When you let your muscles go loose, the bio-feedback is then communicating, "The danger is over now, I don't need to be ready for anything . Your brain responds with 'OK – I'll stop the stress hormones.'

M = Muscles

Check for any tightness or tension in your muscles, and let those muscles go limp, floppy and relaxed.

Finally, as we have discussed in previous chapters, your thoughts will determine what you will ultimately feel. If you are having thoughts that are about fear, catastrophe, not coping – those thoughts will stimulate feelings that will include fearfulness, loss of control and overwhelment. It can be difficult to think at all in the middle of an anxiety or panic attack and it can be impossible to try to find positive thoughts when you are being flooded by stress hormones.

No psychologist worth their salt would ask you to do that. What we do ask is that you suspend or disempower the negative thoughts by focussing instead on what we call **Self-Soothing Thoughts** – more neutral thoughts that just help you to settle the physiological responses to stress.

T = Thoughts

Focus on self-soothing, with messages like

'Relax', 'This will pass', 'I can do this', etc.

Say these self-soothing mantras over and over again, like a broken record. Combined with your slower breathing and relaxed muscles, you should be feeling significantly better in just a few minutes.

The B-M-T model imitates exactly what happens naturally when our nervous system is working properly, that is, when it is able to return naturally to a relaxed state, following arousal in the fight or flight state.

Have you ever had the experience of having a near-hit in your car (I don't know why we tend to say 'near-miss' ; 'I nearly missed, but didn't miss' : Isn't that a hit?) when you nearly hit someone else? Or maybe you just avoided something potentially serious, like jumping out of the way of a run-away horse?

At the time, you would have been experiencing all the signs of being in fight or flight: rapid breathing, rapid heart rate, tense muscles – but once you were aware that danger had been avoided and that you were safe, what do we tend to do naturally? Mostly we take a **deep breath,** we **slump** our bodies, and we **self-soothe** by saying something like 'OMG – thank goodness no-one was hurt.' Then over time, our nervous system returns to its normal relaxed state.

For people with chronic anxiety, it is as though the button is jammed on the arousal side of their nervous system and they find it impossible to move from the sympathetic (arousal) back to the parasympathetic (calming) system. B-M-T provides a quick and discrete pathway. Relaxation CDs can also be very helpful in assisting the brains of chronic anxiety sufferers to settle the fight or flight response and to remember what it feels like to be relaxed.

Before going on to the next technique for settling anxious or negative thoughts and feelings, I just want to say a little more about breathing. Obviously breathing is a fundamental part of living. It is an important part of many ancient traditions and therapies such as yoga and meditation and more recent psychological therapies including relaxation skills training, hypnosis and mindfulness. It is easy to do, it costs nothing, you can do it anywhere without drawing attention to yourself and it can produce almost instant relief. Remember, just as with the B-M-T exercise, slowing your breathing is activating your parasympathetic or the *calming* part of your nervous system (the opposite to the sympathetic nervous system which is your fight or flight reflex).

I find that just taking time during a busy schedule to check in with my breathing can provide enormous relief and grounding. If I have had a particularly challenging session with a client, or found their story distressing, I will sometimes take time to do a short breathing exercise. I find it helps

To Settle Flight or Flight Reflex:

BMT

1. Breathing

Slow your breathing rate down. Breathe in-2-3 through the nose and out-2-3 through the mouth.

2. Muscles

Let your muscles go completely loose and floppy.

3. Thoughts

STOP negative thoughts - focus on SELF-SOOTHING, eg. repeat like a broken record things like "Calm down", "Relax", "This will pass", "You can do it", etc.

to settle me ready for the next client. Whenever you feel that you have been rushing, or feel stressed, - any time that you literally want to 'take a breather' you can - by practising slowing and deepening your breathing. This works particularly well with what is known as 'diaphragmatic breathing', which is breathing that causes your abdomen to push out rather than for your chest to rise up.

Abdominal Breathing Technique
Try to practise this technique twice a day (start and end of the day is good), or use it whenever you are feeling stressed, anxious, experiencing pain, or negative emotion, or just need to take a breather

- Lie down or sit comfortably in a chair and remove any distractions
- Place one hand on your chest and the other on your abdomen
- When you take a deep breath in, the hand on your abdomen should rise higher than the one on your chest. This will confirm that your diaphragm is pulling air in to the lower parts of your lungs.
- Exhale through the mouth and then take a slow, deep breath in through your nose and hold it for a count of 4 or 5 if you can
- Slowly exhale through your mouth to a count of 7 or 8 and then gently contract your tummy muscles to expel any remaining air from your lungs.
- Repeat this cycle four more times – that's a total of 5 deep breaths.

Cognitive-behavioural Therapy (CBT)
Cognitive-behavioural Therapy (CBT) is the therapy currently favoured by our medico-legal system in Australia for the treatment of depression and anxiety. This is largely due to the ability of the therapy to be scientifically measured in randomised controlled trials. As its name implies, the therapy involves two types of strategies: cognitive strategies and behavioural strategies. Cognitive strategies involve becoming familiar with the thoughts, beliefs and attitudes that lead to us feeling bad and changing them to be more realistic and less negative. Behavioural strategies involve doing things that reduce the impact of the negative thoughts and emotions, for example, relaxation techniques, problem-solving skills and assertiveness skills. CBT tends to focus on the client's present experiences rather than on past experiences.

CBT practitioners will assist their clients to evaluate their thoughts, emotions and behaviours using Beck's ***Cognitive Distortions***, another way of saying **'thinking errors.'** CBT is based on the idea that it is not so much an *event* that causes us distress, rather it is our *thoughts about the event*. This can be illustrated by **CBT's A-B-C model of thinking**, where:

A   stands for the **A**ctivating Event – the situation

B   stands for your **B**elief about the Event – or your explanation; and

C   stands for the **C**onsequences – usually feelings and behaviours in response to the event

If I am walking down the street, for example, and a friend passes by me without acknowledging me (ACTIVATING EVENT)

and I have the thought 'Oh, my gosh, Sue just completely ignored me. I must have done something to upset her.' (BELIEF)

that thought will lead to uncomfortable emotion. I am likely to feel confused, hurt, upset, worried and may ruminate on the experience for hours, possibly days and I may avoid contact with Sue in the meantime. (CONSEQUENCES)

CBT would encourage me to consider the *validity* of that thought. Where is the evidence? Is there an alternative possible explanation for Sue's behaviour?

If I have the thought that 'Sue just walked past me without saying hello. Perhaps she has a lot on her mind and didn't see me.' (D = DISPUTING BELIEF)

It is likely that I am going to feel less distressed. (E = EFFECT)

The common thinking errors that the founders of CBT identified are:

1. **Catastrophising**

    When you jump to the worst case scenario and predict negative things for the future.

2. **Black and White Thinking/Perfectionism**

    When you think in extremes, there are no shades of grey: something is either good or bad; right or wrong.

3. **Mind Reading**

    When you assume you know what someone else is thinking and you generally believe others are thinking *badly* about you.

4. **Overgeneralising**

    When you make a rule or label based on either limited information or on a single event, for example, labelling yourself as a bad mother because you forgot to pack your child's swimwear for school sports, or labelling yourself as a bad driver because you had one accident, or having a rule to never eat Chinese food because you had a bad experience once.

5. Exaggerating

When you use words that are extreme and make things seem worse than they are, for example the words should, never, always, must. 'My husband never does anything to help', 'I always mess things up'.

6. Filtering

When you filter out any positive events or experiences, or your strengths and focus your attention on negative events, your weaknesses and the difficulties in your life.

7. Self-blame

When you automatically blame yourself when things go wrong, or take responsibility for things that are not in your control, for example, 'My husband didn't want to have sex last night. I think he finds me unattractive.' 'Jenny was so quiet at the dinner party on Saturday night, I must have made her feel nervous.'

8. Asking Questions that have no Answers

When you ask questions that cannot be answered and serve only to cause you distress, such as 'Why me?', 'How long am I going to feel depressed?'

We all routinely make some of the above thinking errors, but when we are depressed we tend to make them more frequently. Cognitive-behavioural therapy works to increase your knowledge of the thinking errors you commonly make and to assist you in actively intervening in irrational or unhelpful thoughts by disputing them. By reducing the intensity of your thoughts, you reduce the intensity of negative emotions.

Whilst you are learning to recognise the thinking errors you make, the elastic band or wrist band can be a useful aid in focussing your attention.

Many aspects of CBT are incorporated into other therapies mentioned in this section and because there has already been a great deal written about CBT approaches to negative thinking and depression, I am not going to elaborate further on this particular therapy. If you would like to know more about CBT theory and strategies, please refer to the recommended reading at the end of the book.

Thought-Field Therapy (TFT), Emotional Freedom Technique (EFT), Tapping

I have always had an interest in natural medicine and what is now called Integrative Medicine – an approach that is holistic, wellness rather than illness focussed, combining the best of bio-medicine and alternative or complementary medicine. For several years I was Principal of a Complementary Medicine Clinic, that brought together a range of practitioners in modalities including naturopathy, myotherapy, massage therapy, psychology, occupational therapy, acupuncture and Traditional Chinese Medicine. We offered holistic care for our patients within a relaxed, nurturing environment, where appointment times were generous and practitioners worked in collaboration with their patients and medical practitioners to get the best health outcomes. During my time at this clinic, I learned about Chinese medicine, the meridian points and how energy or qi (pronounced chi) works in the body.

I subsequently trained in a technique called 'Thought-Field-Therapy', which was developed by an American clinical psychologist, Dr Roger Callahan, and based on the fields of acupuncture and kinesiology.

Kinesiology literally means 'the study of movement'. It incorporates biofeedback from muscle testing with both Western (anatomy, physiology) and Eastern medicine practices (acupressure and the meridian system) to restore balance.

When I did TFT training early in 2006, it was generally not well known, and without the benefit of the contributions of quantum physics, epigenetics and neuroscience, it was mostly regarded with suspicion or mocked by Western, orthodox medicine practitioners.

The treatment, which is quick and effective, is based on re-setting the body's bioenergy field through tapping with your fingers on specific points on the face and body, which are located along energy meridians.

Dr Callahan discovered this approach after working with a client called Mary, a mother of two in her late thirties, who had suffered a severe and debilitating water phobia since infancy. She was unable to take a bath or to bathe her children, she could not drive along the coast and see the ocean. Whenever it rained she became absolutely terrified and could not leave her home. Dr Callahan worked with Mary unsuccessfully for more than a year using conventional psychological therapies. Then one day as Mary was sitting uncomfortably in Dr Callahan's backyard, in sight of the swimming pool, he asked her where she felt the discomfort and she replied; 'I feel it in the pit of my stomach. Every time I look at or think of water I feel it right here in my stomach.'[1]

Although not professionally trained, Dr Callahan had an interest in and some understanding of Chinese Medicine and meridian points and he knew that a spot directly under the eye was the location of an end point to the stomach meridian.

He asked Mary to think about her fear of the water and to use two fingers to tap firmly under her eye. After just two minutes of tapping, Mary stopped, looked at her therapist and exclaimed, 'It's gone!' Dr Callahan admits that he didn't believe her, but adds, 'Before I could say another word, Mary sprang from her chair and began running toward the swimming pool. She was smiling, even laughing – and picking up speed......

At pool's edge, Mary gazed briefly at her reflection, then bent down and splashed water on her face.'[2] Later that evening Mary waded out into the ocean until she was waist deep in water. Her fear had completely gone.

I had a similarly amazing experience in my own clinic with TFT when I was working with an adult victim of childhood sexual abuse. The woman, in her fifties, disclosed that she had never talked about this before to anyone – she had been carrying these distressing memories around with her for most of her life.

The perpetrator of her abuse had been a family member with whom she still had contact at family gatherings. The memories of the abuse were becoming more and more distressing and affecting her relationships with her husband, her children and her mother. I asked her to take a moment to tune her mind in to the assault experiences and to rate it on a scale of 0 – 10 where 0 indicated no distress and 10 = overwhelming distress – she rated her distress level at 10. We began tapping in a sequence that was appropriate for trauma. After round 1, her distress was down to a 6 out of 10. After round 2 she said, 'It's difficult for me to get it in to my mind. It's gone. I don't feel anything.' After just a couple of minutes, fifty years of distress and suffering had been erased! She left my consulting room elated, saying she had never felt so good in all her life.

At the time, I fully expected to hear from her in a couple of days, to tell me that she was experiencing distressing memories again, but when we met again a couple of weeks later she was still completely free of any negative emotion about the abusive events.

TFT does not remove the memories, just the emotion that they carry. This client had even been able to attend a family gathering and had no triggering of any negative emotion. She remains completely free of any distress seven years later.

Thought-Field-Therapy was further developed by a man called Gary Craig, who was concerned about the strict licensing of TFT which limited its availability to mostly middle-class health professionals, who had to be credentialed before they could use the therapy with clients. Craig simplified Dr Callahan's techniques and published them on the world wide web, so that anyone could become familiar with and use the technique for themselves without the need to consult a therapist.

More recently, tapping has become popularised through the work of Nick Ortner and his very successful book *The Tapping Solution*. Nick has simplified the technique once again, without, it seems, any loss of power. Here is an outline of how it works:

Emotional Freedom Technique (EFT)

1. Tune your thoughts in to the distressing event and rate it on a scale of between 0 = no distress and 10 = overwhelming distress. (This scale is called the Subjective Units of Distress Scale – SUDS).

2. Set the problem statement by stating the problem in this way:

   'Even though (I feel hurt by my boss's comments) I fully and completely accept myself'. At the same time, tap with the two fingers of your dominant hand on a position on the side of the other hand called the Karate Chop Point. Continue tapping on this point whilst you repeat this statement a further two times.

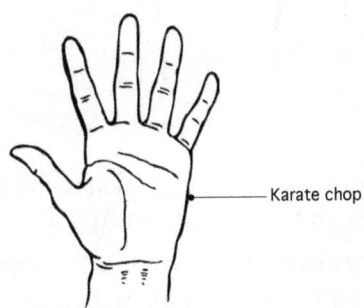

3. Repeat key points of the statement (e.g. feel hurt….; boss's comments) as you tap through the points in the order illustrated below:

> 1. Between the eyes
> 2. At the end of the eyes
> 3. Under the eyes
> 4. Under the nose
> 5. On the chin
> 6. Under the collar bone
> 7. Under the arms
> 8. On top of the head

Diagram - Tapping through the meridian points

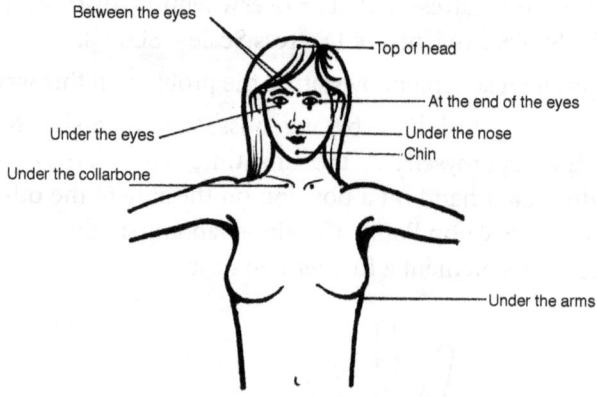

4. Take a deep breath in and out. Tune in again to the cause of your distress and rate it once again on the scale of 0 to 10.
5. If you are still experiencing distress, repeat the steps again, and again if necessary, until you find relief and your SUDS score drops to at least a 2.

One of the things I really like about this therapy, and the reason I use it with sexual assault victims in particular, is that it does not require the victim to tell their story, which can be incredibly upsetting and retraumatising. At worst, the client will be required to tune in to the distressing feelings for a few minutes.

Compare this to having to talk about very personal distressing events for hours in the therapist's consulting rooms. I have also used this technique successfully with anxiety and phobias and children in particular seem to embrace it. I understand that psychologists, doctors and health and aid workers who assist in critical incidents overseas, are now being trained to use tapping with victims of natural and other disasters as a first aid intervention. For more information on TFT, EFT and tapping refer to the suggested reading at the end of the book.

Mindfulness and Acceptance and Commitment Therapy (ACT)

Acceptance and Commitment Therapy (ACT) was developed in the late 1980s by psychologist Steven Hayes of University of Nevada and his two colleagues Kirk Strosahl and Kelly Wilson. It has probably only been widely used by Australian psychologists over the last ten years. ACT aims to assist clients to live full and meaningful lives, whilst effectively managing difficult and painful circumstances that inevitably arise, rather than avoiding or struggling with them.

ACT aims to move people away from the problems represented by the acronym **FEAR,** so that they can take **ACT**ion:

F	fusion with your thoughts
E	evaluation of experience
A	avoidance of your experience
R	reason-giving for your behaviour

A	Accept your reactions and be present
C	Choose a valued direction
T	Take action

ACT is based on the following six core principles:-

1. Cognitive Defusion - reducing the impact of painful or unpleasant thoughts, so they have less influence over your behaviour
2. Acceptance or Expansion – giving space to unpleasant feelings rather than suppressing or struggling with them.
3. Contact with the Present Moment or Connection – being present in the here and now
4. Observing the Self – stepping out of the experience of negative emotions and being an observer of them
5. Values – becoming clear about the values that matter to you and give your life meaning
6. Committed action – taking action that is motivated by your values.

Although ACT is considered a relatively new therapy, particularly in Australia, you may already see some similarities between the six principles outlined above and some of the key factors for living a more meaningful life outlined by the researchers into happiness.

Currently ACT is a very popular therapy. It is used by many Australian psychologists partly because, like Cognitive-behavioural Therapy (CBT), the most popular therapy for treatment of depression and anxiety, ACT has been rigorously scientifically tested. This means that much of the treatment has been standardised, which makes measuring and validating outcomes easier, particularly if the treatment is being funded by government.

I plan to introduce you to just a couple of techniques utilised by ACT therapists that are quick and easy to learn and practise and are designed to give you prompt relief from uncomfortable thoughts and feelings. For more detailed information on Mindfulness and ACT, please refer to the suggested readings at the end of the book.

Technique 1 - I AM HAVING THE THOUGHT THAT....

This technique is designed to achieve ACT's first goal, that of cognitive defusion. When we are stressed or anxious, often we take the negative thoughts that we are having as being real and the truth, rather than an interpretation or perception. For example, if I am having the thought 'I am a bad mother', I am likely to be feeling pretty wretched – possibly ashamed, upset, sad, disappointed, guilty, useless. Perhaps I had that thought after forgetting to pick something up for one of my children. My identity, my sense of myself has become 'fused' with the thought and so I feel awful. But by inserting the words, *I am having the thought that*....(I am a bad mother) puts some distance between the thoughts and ME. It's like stepping back just a little from the thought. I can step back even a little further if I then combine defusing with observing and say: *I notice I am having the thought that...*(I am a bad mother).

The aim of defusion is not to avoid or to get rid of a thought, but simply to reduce its impact or power by seeing it as just a collection of words in a sentence - not a universal truth. If you suffer from depression and anxiety, this technique can be very helpful as you practice your BMT and say 'I notice I am having the thought that something terrible is going to happen', or 'I notice I am having the thought that I am going to have a heart attack.'

It sounds like such a simple thing to do, it's hard to imagine that it could have much impact, but it does – and I know that many of my clients have gained enormous relief quite quickly by using this technique.

Technique 2 - MINDFULNESS

Mindfulness, which has come from Buddhist philosophy and contemplative practice, has many different definitions here in the West, depending on the context in which it is used. In his very popular and successful book on ACT, Russ Harris, defines mindfulness as 'consciously bringing awareness to your here-and-now experience, with openness, receptiveness, and interest.'[3] Michael Anderson, a psychologist who teaches Mindfulness Practice to psychologists in Australia says that mindfulness is hard to define to someone who has not had experience of it. He says it is a little like trying to define the taste of an orange to someone who has never eaten one, but he goes on to define it this way; 'Mindfulness is the capacity to maintain awareness of your current experience without the limitations of your past experiences and your expectations of how things should or shouldn't be.'[4] Buddhists will often refer to the 'emptiness' of things, or to the theory and practice of 'non-attachment' – an acceptance of what is, without evaluating or trying to change it.

I have already referred to the work of Jon Kabat-Zinn who has been very successful in reducing the impact of the symptoms of depression and anxiety for his clients at the stress clinic that he established.

His definition of mindfulness is: 'Mindfulness means paying attention in a particular way: on purpose, in the present moment, and nonjudgmentally. This kind of attention nurtures greater awareness, clarity, and acceptance of present-moment reality.'[5] Jon has written several excellent easy to read books on mindfulness, many include exercises to undertake and he has produced several Mindfulness CDs, which can be purchased on-line.

So, essentially mindfulness is about being present to what is happening, what you are thinking and what you are feeling, without evaluating, without struggling; it is about acceptance, non-judgement and the impermeance of things. It's about letting things BE.

Exercises in Mindfulness

1. Mindful sitting

   This is a great introduction exercise for those of you who may not have had any meditation or mindfulness experience. Sit yourself in a comfortable chair, with your arms on the sides of the chair or rested in your lap, feet flat on the ground and place yourself in front of a clock. For one minute, place your full attention on your breathing, and only your breathing. Don't try to judge or change it, just observe it, feel it, pay attention to every detail. The in breath, the out breath, is the air warm or cold as it enters your nose? Is your chest, your tummy rising and falling with each breath?

2. Mindful walking

   I personally love mindful walking practice. I have never been too good at meditation, although I wish I could be, because its benefits are so well established in the scientific literature. Unfortunately I have ants in my pants and find it hard to be still for any length of time. Instead, I like to walk barefoot and mindfully on my local beach, and find it particularly refreshing and energising, especially at the end of a long day consulting.

   Take your shoes off, if that is possible, and feel the connection of your body through your feet to the ground or the floor. Take a deep breath in and focus your attention on your surroundings. Remember to pay attention to each of the senses. What can you see? What can you hear? What can you taste? What can you feel? As you begin to walk bring your awareness to the shifting weight of your body from your left to your right leg, focus your attention on the sensations through your feet, up your legs, into your body. Notice what is happening with your arms. If any thoughts arise, just let them float away, and bring your attention back to the sensations within your body, in contact with the earth.

   Walk slowly, rhythmically. Notice your breath. Has it changed in any way since you started walking? Are the rhythms of your breath lining up with the rhythm of your steps? When you come to the end of your walk, take a moment to be still and feel the sensations of that stillness throughout your body. Be aware of your breath and be appreciative of the time you have just spent in the practice of mindfulness before returning to your normal awareness and activity.

Reaching for a Better Thought or Feeling

This technique has come from the work of Abraham as written by Esther and Jerry Hicks and it is very similar to some cognitive-behavioural therapies, (disputing negative cognitions or thoughts). These strategies are designed to challenge your immediate thoughts and consequent negative feelings and to shift you one thought at a time from extreme negative thoughts and feelings to less negative, neutral or positive thoughts and feelings. I have used this technique successfully with many of my clients and I use it regularly for myself, particularly when I feel stuck around something, or when I know I am reacting to old hurts and sensitivities.

This is a written exercise, so you will need an exercise book, or a piece of lined A4 paper. Start where you are right now in relation to the issue of concern to you and write this at the top of the page:

EXAMPLE:

WHERE I AM NOW:

I am feeling unloved and unwanted because no-one has been in touch with me this week.

Next identify what you are feeling from the scale of emotions on page 76. Let's say you rate this feeling as No 21 - Insecurity/Guilt/Unworthiness - an extremely low vibrational frequency.

Now, at the bottom of your page, I want you to write a statement about how you would *prefer* to feel in relation to this matter:-

WHERE I WOULD PREFER TO BE:

I would prefer to feel loved and appreciated.

You identify that if you were feeling this, it would rate as No 1 on the emotional scale - Joy/Empowerment/Freedom/Love/Appreciation.

Now, we know that when you are subsumed with powerful and negative emotions it is way too hard to try and get to feeling more positive and loving. So what we are going to do instead, is to try to move ourselves one step at a time away from where we are now, towards where we would prefer to be. Understand that this process may take more than one sitting with this exercise

Scale of Emotions

From *Ask and It Is Given* - **Esther and Jerry Hicks**

1. Joy/Empowerment/Freedom/Love/Appreciation
2. Passion
3. Enthusiasm/Eagerness/Happiness
4. Positive Expectation/Belief
5. Optimism
6. Hopefulness
7. Contentment
8. Boredom
9. Pessimism
10. Frustration/Irritation/Impatience
11. Overwhelment
12. Disappointment
13. Doubt
14. Worry
15. Blame
16. Discouragement
17. Anger
18. Revenge
19. Hatred/Rage
20. Jealousy
21. Insecurity/Guilt/Unworthiness
22. Fear/Grief/Depression/Despair/Powerlessness

– it could take days, or weeks, but the aim is to reach for some relief from the distressing emotions and lift your vibrational frequency.

So, try to find a statement in relation to the situation, that will stand in contrast to the initial thought and provide some sense of relief. For example:

Just because I haven't heard from people this week, doesn't mean that people don't care about me.

So now you might rate this new thought and feelings it generates as more like No 16 – Discouragement. You have moved yourself several points up the scale and changed your vibrational frequency as a result with just one change in your thinking.

Then you may remember that actually a couple of friends did make contact during the past week. If so you may write:

Actually, my friend Jenny visited me last week and Josie texted me twice.

Now you can rate how you are feeling as being closer to No 13 Doubt and again you have moved yourself several points higher on the emotional scale. In just two thoughts you have moved yourself from the bottom of the emotional scale to somewhere in the middle – and it is likely that you will be feeling the relief of that change, feeling less intensity and more hopeful.

Continue with this process for as long as you feel you need to, or until you are satisfied with the level of relief you can achieve around the particular issue .

It is not necessary to move yourself to the very top of the scale, it is only necessary that you achieve a sense of relief and hope. Over time, your completed page may look like this:-

---

Where I am NOW:

I am feeling unloved and unwanted because no-one has been in touch with me this week.

    Just because I haven't heard from people this week doesn't mean people don't care about me.

    My friend Jenny visited me last week and Josie texted me twice

    I usually hear from most of my friends by text pretty regularly

    Mum and Dad are away on holidays and my best friend is at a Conference this week

I guess many of the people I hear from have been busy this week

I suppose I could always ring or go visit someone – I don't have to wait for them

I do have friends and family who care about me

I don't feel so cut off now

I am surrounded by photos of people who are special to me

I am lucky to have so many people who care about me

Where I would prefer to be in relation to this issue:

I feel loved and appreciated.

I hope you find relief in the practice of these exercises. In the chapters to follow, I will be introducing you to more techniques for moving away from unwanted, unpleasant thoughts, feelings and experiences, towards more of what you would like to have in your life - happiness, connection, meaning and purpose. We will be doing exercises that are designed for you to get to know yourself, what you really want for your life, what you value, what your primary character strengths are and how you can maintain positive physical, emotional and spiritual health.

(Endnotes)
1. Callahan, Roger J. *Tapping the Healer Within*. (New York:McGraw Hill, 2001).
2. Ibid
3. Harris, R. *The Happiness Trap - How to Stop Struggling and Start Living*. (USA:Trumpeter, 2008).
4. Anderson, M. *Mindfulness Practice*. (Aust: The Australian Institute of Emotional Intelligence, 2004).
5. Kabat-Zinn, J. *Wherever You Go There You Are - Mindfulness Meditation in Everyday Life*. (USA: Hyperion, 2005).

Chapter 6 - Focus Attention on What You DO Want, Not on What You DON'T Want

"You have to count on living every single day in a way you believe will make you feel good about your life – so that if it were over tomorrow, you'd be content with yourself."

Jane Seymour

Quantum physics research shows us that reduced down to its smallest component, all matter in the universe, including us, is made up of vibrating energy and that that energy vibrates at different rates or frequencies. It is also true in physics that like attracts like and that this principle can be applied to how we live our lives. So, if we are thinking worrying or negative thoughts, we will attract things, people, and experiences that match the vibration of that negativity . Conversely, if we are thinking and feeling positive emotions, we are a vibrational match for more positive emotions and experiences. Esther and Jerry Hicks have written about what they call the 'Law of Attraction' in a number of books and this universal and inviolable principle was the subject of a film called *The Secret* produced by an Australian woman Rhonda Byrne.

Simply put, whatever you put your attention on GROWS, so best to put your attention on what you *do want*, rather than what you *don't want* and on positive rather than negative emotions and thoughts.

As a psychologist, I see many unhappy people and I am troubled by how young some of my clients are when they experience their first episode of depression or crippling anxiety. It has become routine for parents to bring their unhappy children to specialists – psychologists, paediatricians, school counsellors, etc. and they do so with the best of intentions. But I can't help feeling that my own profession is contributing to the growing incidence of depression and anxiety by talking about it so much, by focussing so much attention on negative emotions and experiences and by pathologising normal emotions such as sadness, grief, disappointment and frustration. By focussing attention on what is *wrong*, we may be complicit in obscuring from our clients what is *right* in their lives - distracting them from a connection to their inherent knowledges, competencies and skills and therefore their confidence to effectively manage their emotions and lives.

Mother Teresa seemed to intuitively understand the power of paying attention and giving energy to what you want, rather than what you don't want, when she said:

> 'I will never attend an anti-war rally. If you have a peace rally, invite me.'
>
> *Mother Teresa*

I remember a time in April 1992, when Yassar Arafat (the then leader of the Palestine Liberation Organisation) was on a plane that went missing and was subsequently found to have crashed in the Libyan desert during a sandstorm. Before it was even clear what had happened, Western journalists and media outlets started releasing stories about his unconfirmed death. I still recall the extreme distress of Yassar Arafat's supporters. They were horrified and angry that in the hours between the plane being overdue and the wreckage being discovered and Mr Arafat found alive, Westerners were reporting a likely negative outcome. The Arab people believed it was bad to predict a negative outcome; that if you thought such things they would come true. They pleaded with Western journalists to stop their negative reporting and change their thoughts about predicting Mr Arafat's safety.

This story and Mother Teresa's quote remind me to never be anti anything, because it is giving attention to what you don't want more of, but always to be pro-active instead. For example, rather than anti-whaling, or anti-logging in our forests, be pro-conservation; instead of being anti-domestic violence, be pro-safety for women and children; instead of anti-discrimination, be pro-inclusiveness, acceptance, tolerance. Once you start to understand and consider the power of this shift, it will amaze you to notice just how often we in the Western world focus on what we don't want.

When I start work with a newly referred client, I spend the first session hearing about 'the problem(s)' of their life. For someone with a big history and many problems this may take two sessions, but fairly soon, I actively encourage them to move away from where they are to where they want to be by asking them 'What would you prefer your life to be like?' and their answers help me to know what the goal of therapy is. So, rather than focussing on what is wrong with your life and all the problems you perceive within it, let's spend some time now getting clear around what you would really like your life to

Focus Attention on What You DO Want, Not on What You DON'T Want

look like. If you had a magic wand, or you came across a genie from a lamp, who could grant all your wishes, what would you wish for?

I want you to approach the exercise on the next page as if there were absolutely no constraints or limitations, no BUTS. This is an exercise in dreaming: fantasizing about all the things your heart desires. Try to include as much detail as you can, as if you were ordering this life from an online 'Order Your Ideal Life Here' store. You wouldn't want to have to send it back, because you had forgotten an important detail. 'Oh, you sent me a man who likes to go fishing and hunting and shooting and then likes to eat the animals he has killed by throwing them on the barby. Did I forget to tell you that my ideal man shares my commitment to being vegetarian? I didn't? Oh! What do you mean you have a no-returns policy?'

So, time to get clear about what your Ideal World looks like…

My Ideal World

What am I doing?

Where am I living?

Who am I with?

What things are around me?

How am I feeling?

OK, so now I hope you are clearer about what you would prefer to have in your life. Do you believe that it is possible for you to have this? Any part of it? I hope you said yes, because it is not going to come to you if you hold beliefs that are directly opposed to it.

Techniques for helping you to stay focussed on what you DO want rather than what you DON'T

State an Intention

OK, so first step is to state an intention, or you could call it goal-setting. What is the most important aspect of the life you would prefer to be leading? Is it a relationship, financial or occupational success, is it an improved health outcome? Whatever it is I want you to state it in the present tense as an intention, for example:

"It is my intention to meet my ideal partner within the next twelve months."

"It is my intention to lose ten kilos before my daughter's wedding next spring."

"It is my intention to be promoted to Manager of my division within three months of my next performance appraisal."

Use Visual Cues

Many people find visual cues extremely helpful when they are working towards manifesting a new intention in their lives. You may have heard of 'Vision Boards', which are essentially poster boards with pictures, words, and graphics depicting the object of your desire. It is then placed in a prominent position where you can focus your attention on it regularly (I like the bedroom wall on the opposite wall from where I sleep, so I can focus my attention on what I want first thing in the morning and last thing at night – remember these are the two times when our brain waves are slower, and more open to suggestion). You can have a lot of fun with this; invite friends over to do it together, raid your children's textas, glitter, stickers, cut out pictures from magazines, use photographs, etc. Let your creative talents run wild.

I have used a vision board twice in my life and at the time I did them I really wasn't too sure about it; I was a bit sceptical. The first time was when my former husband and I wanted to leave where we were living and return to mainland Australia so we could be closer to our families. Our dream was to build our own home on a few acres in the countryside. On a large green poster board I drew a picture of a home with a verandah around it, a long driveway leading up to it, paddocks each side of the road, with horses, sheep, and chickens. At first the poster board was placed on the wall at the house we were living in at the time, but then we were transferred to another home and it was packed into a box with many other things that subsequently were not unpacked for years. To tell you the truth, I never gave it another thought. Life went on as usual and after six months in this new location, we moved again, this time back to the mainland and on to a few acres that we had fallen in love with whilst visiting the area on holiday. We subsequently built our own home. The children grew up, my marriage ended, and the children and I moved into town for two years. I eventually moved back out to the property and only a couple of years ago I finally unpacked the box in which I had placed the Vision Board I had made all those years ago. I unrolled it and felt absolutely stunned – the drawing on the poster board was the image of the house and property on which I was now living! A house with a verandah, long winding driveway with paddocks either side and with sheep and chickens.

The second occasion on which I did a Vision Board occurred ten years after my divorce. I had started to think about having a partner in my life once again, but I wanted to make sure this time that I had my Ideal Partner. I cut a picture out of a magazine of a tall, dark and handsome man with a captain's hat on, at the wheel of a boat. I stated the intention that 'I now have a man who is kind, considerate, loyal, responsible and financially independent'. My friends at the time used to laugh and say, 'Tess, he doesn't exist! You are being way too fussy". I would reply that I was willing to wait to attract the best and would remain on my own rather than compromise. I constructed my Vision board on 25th August 2008 , and on 25th July 2009 I met the man in my Vision Board.

Not only does he look uncannily like the man at the wheel of the boat, he has every quality that I had hoped for (and more). This has been the most wonderfully nurturing, supportive and fulfilling relationship I have ever experienced and I have absolutely no doubt that it will continue to be so. Oh, and once I got to know him a little better he told me that as a child he constantly wore a captain's hat around , he doesn't really know why!

Another way of keeping yourself focussed on your object of intention is to post sticky notes around the place – on the bathroom mirror, on the dashboard of the car, inside your purse or wallet, on the inside cover of your diary, etc. It is best to write your notes as affirmations (see over) in present tense.

Affirmations

Remember from the early chapters that our thoughts can create our reality and that this is supported by the evidence from the new science of neuroplasticity. We have the power to reshape our brains by changing our thoughts and mentally rehearsing what we want rather than what we don't want. We are involved in so much 'monkey chatter', that we talk to ourselves constantly. It has been estimated that we have between twelve thousand and sixty thousand thoughts each day and that as much as seventy to eighty per cent of those thoughts are negative. Imagine the depth of the groove that this is creating in the neural pathways of your brain.

In June 2006 Pastor Will Bowen of the Christ Church Unity in Kansas City set up a challenge for the members of his congregation when he handed each one of them a purple wristband and told them to put it on their wrist. He then asked that for the next twenty-one days, each time they complained, they should transfer the band from the wrist it was on to the other one. Remember my elastic band therapy for increasing awareness and reducing the incidence of negative thinking? Well, this is doing much the same thing.

The goal was to try to have his parishioners complaint-free for twenty-one days – the time it takes to replace an old habit with a new habit, or to extinguish an old neural pathway and create a new one.

Pastor Bowen's idea has taken off and now more than ten million purple wristbands have been sold worldwide! Visit www.acomplaintfreeworld.com for more information or to get bracelets.

Affirmations are positive statements that are framed in the present tense and reflect your stated intention about what you want or what you would prefer. For example, if you are struggling with finances and would like more money to come into your life, don't be focussed on what you don't want (the lack of money), focus on what you *do* want, e.g.:

Rather than:
- I wish I could afford to get ....
- Maybe I can get that new dress when it comes on sale
- How come other people seem to be able to have annual holidays?

Affirm what it is you do want, as if it were already happening
- I now have enough money to meet all my needs and wants
- I deserve an abundance of all things positive
- All my bills are paid on time

Try to incorporate your affirming statements into other routines within your life. For example, I tend to use rhyming affirmations whilst I am swimming and counting laps in the pool. So Lap One – I'm having fun; Lap Two - I love you; Lap Three – I feel free; Lap Four – I adore my life; Lap Five – I'm so alive; etc. Or I say affirmations in rhythm with the steps of my walking. You could sing them if you prefer. For more on affirmations I recommend Louise Hay's book *Heal Your Life*.

Gratitude

One of the quickest ways of moving yourself away from focussing attention of what is not right in your life, is to pay attention to all that is right in your life. When people are depressed, they find it difficult to be able to find anything to be grateful for, but with consistent practice, there is always something, no matter how little or insignificant it may seem. Remember, the walk of a thousand miles begins with one step. One technique that I have regularly practised for several years now and one I routinely share with my patients is to take time at the end of every day to find five things to be grateful for about that day.

I recommend that you buy an inexpensive day-to-a-page diary at the start of each new year and use this to make your entries. What I suggest to my clients is that at the end of each day, just before going to bed, you write down five things that were good about the day you have just lived. Even if you are suffering depression, anxiety, or just not in a good place right now, I am certain that you can find five things to be appreciative of, for example,:

- I am grateful to have vision so that I can be writing this
- I am grateful to live in a country that is safe and has no wars
- I am grateful to have a roof over my head tonight
- I am grateful for my warm blankets
- I am grateful for the food I ate today

Why not try it yourself? By consistently paying attention to what is right and good in your life on a daily basis, you are changing your vibrational alignment to be more in tune with what you want and helping to lay down new and more positive neural pathways. Remember, by deliberately thinking about more positive things and establishing these new neural pathways, you are restructuring your brain to be more active in the left frontal lobe (the centre of positive emotion) and less active in the right frontal lobe (the region for experiencing negative emotion).

In addition, doing this exercise just prior to falling asleep sets you up to end the day and drift off in a positive frame of mind and emotional state, ready in the morning for the new day ahead.

Here's a sample from my own gratitude journal:

> I am grateful that:
>
> I arrived home safely
>
> I enjoyed a lovely meal tonight
>
> It was a warm, sunny day
>
> I felt I did some good work today

Meditation

The health benefits of meditation have been well studied and shown to contribute to longevity, increased happiness, reduced stress, better relationships, greater energy, less chronic illness, and improved immune function. A study led by Dr Herbert Benson of Harvard Medical School compared the results of two groups. The experimental group regularly practised yoga or meditation; the control group practised no form of relaxation. The results of the experiment were that a range of disease-fighting genes were found to be active within the group of relaxation (yoga or meditation) practitioners, but were not active in the control group members (who practised no form of relaxation). Specifically, the researchers found that genes that protect against pain, high blood pressure, infertility and rheumatoid arthritis were switched on in the members of the relaxation practitioners group, but not in the members of the control group. Dr Benson then had the control group start practising relaxation methods each day and after just two months he found that genes that help fight inflammation, protect the body from cancer and disease all began to switch on.

Furthermore, ongoing practice of methods such as deep breathing or meditation were found to lead to even further enhanced health benefits, including freedom from arthritic pain, lower blood pressure, healthier hormone levels and improved immune function. [1].

Earlier in the section on the fight or flight reflex (the sympathetic nervous system), I outlined what happens when the stress response is activated and how stress hormones such as adrenalin and cortisol accelerate the heart rate and blood pressure, weaken immunity, and shut down digestion. By contrast, the state of relaxation (the parasympathetic nervous system) promotes the release of feel-good chemicals such as serotonin, which has virtually the opposite effect on our bodies. It lowers our heart rate and blood pressure, boosts immunity and improves digestive function.

I will outline in the chapter dealing with nutrition that serotonin, a neurotransmitter, is present in very high levels in the gastro-intestinal system and has an important impact on the digestive process, which explains why people will often experience upset tummies when they are emotionally upset.

A number of other studies in Australia and overseas have confirmed the beneficial results of relaxation, yoga, or meditative practice on physiological and psychological health. Just fifteen minutes practice a day can cause the positive gene expression identified in the Harvard Medical School experiment. If you are like me and find sitting still and emptying your mind difficult, you could try a relaxation CD, such as the two I have produced (one for daytime and another for night-time) in which you are led through techniques designed to cause a shift from the arousing part of your nervous system across to the relaxation or calming part of your nervous system. These techniques include progressive muscle relaxation, breathing, guided imagery and hypnotic suggestion for feelings of wellbeing and last for about twenty minutes. CDs used in the Harvard Medical School research with the novice relaxation practitioners were also twenty minute CDs using exactly the same techniques. I often find that once my clients have been using the CDs regularly, over time they are able to use the techniques by recalling them to mind themselves whenever the need arises.

For more information on relaxation CDs, refer to the Recommended Reading and Resources section at the end of the book.

There are many different types of meditative practice, yoga and relaxation techniques. I have included here what I believe to be one of the simplest and easiest forms of meditation – Gazing Meditation. You will notice that it is very similar to the experience of "day-dreaming" and I like it because you can do it anywhere at any time and receive immediate benefit in terms of clearing a cluttered mind or uncomfortable emotions and feeling calmer and more relaxed. I have used it whilst sitting in my office chair in between patients in the clinic, sitting in the car (not driving), travelling on public transport, walking through a forest, lying on a beach or looking out the window at home. It can work anywhere.

Gazing Meditation
Wherever you are, sit or lie comfortably, making sure your arms and legs are uncrossed and take a moment to check your breathing. Take three deep

breaths in and out to the count of In-two-three; Hold-two-three; Out-two-three. Now focus your attention on an object within your view. It doesn't matter particularly what it is - whatever catches your eye. Continue to keep your gaze upon the object of your choice without breaking contact (blinking is OK). You may find that after a while your peripheral vision distorts in some way, the object may blur or seem to be vibrating. That's all normal, nothing to worry about. Maintain your unbroken gaze for as long as you wish. When you are ready, bring your focus back in to the room or place you are in and return to your normal activities.

That's it!

Looking at a single object without looking away is known as one-pointed concentration and brings all the benefits of other, more difficult meditations. When I was about twenty-two years old, I went to my first meditation class and the object of our focus was a candle.

I was amazed at how effective this simple meditation was in reducing 'monkey chatter' and settling stress. Choose an object that inspires feelings of peace, tranquillity, compassion, or love. Some kind of light for example, or a photograph or picture of beautiful scenery or someone you love, an object of art or beauty – a statue, a textural cushion, a sculpture. This will enhance your meditative experience.

I hope you find the techniques outlined above helpful to you in maintaining your focus of attention on the things that you do want in your life rather than on the things that you don't. Remember, these strategies are not a prescription; they are suggestions for you to try. Some will resonate and lead to better outcomes for you than others and that's absolutely fine. Just incorporate the ones that you enjoy or that work, and disregard the ones that don't.

(Endnotes)
1. Bhasin MK, Dusek, JA, Chang B-H, Joseph MG, Denninger JW, et al. (2013) Relaxation Response Induces Temporal Transcriptome Changes in Energy Metabolism, Insulin Secretion and Inflammatory Pathways. PLoS ONE 8(5):e62817. Doi: 10.1371/journal.pone.0062817

Chapter 7- Tell a Different Story

Narrative Therapy

This chapter draws on my experience of Narrative Therapy. Narrative therapy is not widely taught to or practised by psychologists in Australia, although there is a moderate amount of interest amongst the profession. I was very fortunate to have been trained by the one of the founders of the therapy, Michael White of the Dulwich Centre in Adelaide. Michael was a gifted therapist and charismatic man, who died suddenly and prematurely in April 2008. His Narrative Therapy is, I believe, not well understood by some health professionals, who often tend to simplify it by assuming that it is about encouraging people to recover from unwellness by telling their stories. Although changing the problem stories of our lives forms part of Narrative Therapy, it is an incredibly rich, sophisticated and complex therapy with roots in philosophy, sociology and psychology. It is considered the therapy of choice for working with Indigenous people and children, and young people tend to embrace it enthusiastically. As a therapist, I find that when I am working within a Narrative perspective, I have to be alert and constantly vigilant in looking for threads of a person's story so that I can assist my client in connecting these threads together to form 'landscapes of identity'.

What is Narrative Therapy? In a nutshell – narrative therapy centres the client as the experts in their own lives; it views the problems that people experience as *separate* to them – the problem is the problem, the client is not the problem, and it assumes that people have many skills, attributes, knowledges, values and beliefs that will assist them to reduce the impact of these problems on their lives. The key principles of Narrative Therapy are:-

- It is respectful and non-blaming
- It centres people as experts in their own lives (not therapists)
- It views problems as separate to people
- It assumes people have many competencies, skills, beliefs, values and abilities
- It takes a position of genuine curiosity (about the life of the client) asking questions to which we (therapists) do not have the answers

There is no prescriptive formula for proceeding in narrative therapy, there are many possible directions and the client is always involved in mapping the direction of the therapeutic journey.

For narrative therapists stories are:-

- Events
- Linked in sequence
- Across time
- According to a plot

Our lives are multi-storied and they are mostly told through conversations. We have stories about our successes, competencies and triumphs, stories about our failures and sadnesses, stories about missed opportunities, stories about people that helped or hurt us. We link certain events of our lives together in a sequence and then draw inferences or attribute meaning to this group of sequenced events. When we do this, we privilege certain information that fits with the story, over information that doesn't. Over time, this can make it difficult for us to even access information about alternative stories to the problem story. For clients who are presenting for counselling, they are often focussed on the problem story(ies) of their lives, for example:-

A client's story of herself as a bad driver:

Imagine that each of the x points below represents an event in the client's history of being a driver. If she is telling the story of herself as a bad driver, she will recall and select parts of the story that fit with the theme (bad driver) and privilege these over other stories that don't fit with the theme (*not* a bad driver).

X	x	x	x	x	x	x
						x = all events
x	**X**	x	x	x		**X = dominant or problem-story plot**
x	x	**X**	**X**	x	**X**	

In the re-telling of the dominant story, alternative stories (such as not being a bad driver) become obscured. In addition, the reflections of others will assist in the story becoming richer and dominant, for example, if the client's husband agrees with her that she is a bad driver. The dominant story will not only affect us in the present, but in the future, (we expect and others expect us to be a bad driver and we will keep selecting evidence that fits with the plot). Therefore the meanings we give to the events of our lives are not neutral in their effects on our lives; they will shape and constitute our lives in the future.

As with Positive Psychology, Narrative Therapy acknowledges that we conduct our lives under the influence of socio-political factors. The context of gender, class, race, culture and sexual preference are all powerful contributors to the plot or theme of our stories.

The goal of Narrative Therapy is to assist clients in remembering or seeking out stories of identity that stand in contrast to the dominant/problem story and help make them 'rich' by collecting as much detail about these alternative stories as possible. Cognitive-behavioural therapists use the strategy of collecting evidence to dispute automatic negative thoughts and attributions, and coming to new, less negative conclusions in the interpretations of the events of our lives.

So, for the client who tells the story of herself being a bad driver, we would invite her to try to remember events that stand in contrast to that story. In other words, can she recall an event that shows her as a good driver? In Narrative Therapy, it is called looking for Unique Outcomes and the goal is to continue gathering up these re-membered contrasting situations in order to enrich the new alternative story of the client as a good driver. There are a number of techniques for assisting clients in this process, but I won't elaborate here. If you are interested to know more about Narrative Therapy, one of the best books ever written as an introduction is by Alice Morgan and called *What is Narrative Therapy*.

Michael White used to encourage us to think about the multi-stories of our lives a bit like a multi-storied building, where the basement is the dominant story of our lives (the problem story – the one that has us seeking help). We become trapped in the basement and don't have access to the other multi-stories of our lives. What we need to do as therapists is to provide scaffolding to allow the client to access those other floors of the building – the alternative stories. Most people know how they would prefer their lives to be and the therapist and client collaborate in collecting evidence of events and beliefs that support that preferred story. Sometimes that can include recruiting others in the collecting of evidence – perhaps family members, work colleagues, teachers, or friends that have experienced you in different ways to the problem story – these people are called Outsider Witnesses.

We are both social and perceiving creatures, we tend to want to draw inferences from the information that comes to us via our senses and brains and we are also influenced by the inferences of others. Our brains are designed to chunk information down into categories - a bit like folders or files on our computers - and sometimes we make these judgements quickly, based on limited information. Or we have made them early in our lives and have not readjusted them to accord with more recent experience.

Have a look at these stories below and after reading them, jot down in a few words your immediate impression of the person in the story. Do you think you would like this person if you were to meet them? There are no right or wrong answers here – I am really just interested in your honest opinion.

Women's Stories Vignettes

>**Jenny** is a single Mum with three children. She works hard but still struggles financially and she worries about how this might affect the children. Once the children are in bed, Jenny sometimes drinks to relieve the stress and she often feels depressed. Her drinking has never gotten in the way of her doing her job or looking after her children, but she doesn't feel good about it and she worries that she is not a good mother and that her children are missing out.

What are your first impressions of Jenny? _____

_____

Would you like Jenny if you met her? Why?/Why not? _____

_____

>**Ruth** is a highly educated professional, who was dux of her school. She has two degrees and two diplomas and she just can't seem to stop learning. She constantly reads non-fiction works, she is currently studying a new post-graduate diploma whilst still working, and her friends say she has a very analytical mind. She has worked as a consultant at very high levels in government.

What are your first impressions of Ruth? _____

Would you like Ruth if you met her? Why?/Why not?_____
_____

Sarah is shy, anxious and worries a lot. She often feels she isn't good enough and that people don't really like her. She doesn't like to go out a lot because she feels uncomfortable in social situations. She has tended to attract men who take advantage of her and confirm her low self-esteem by pointing out her short-comings . **Sarah** suffers from a lack of confidence and low self-esteem. She finds it hard to say NO to people and ends up doing things she often doesn't really have time for.

What are your first impressions of Sarah?_____
_____

Would you like Sarah if you met her? Why?/Why not?_____
_____

Karen has three adult children who adore her. Her youngest child nominated her for a Mother of the Year Award; her eldest child – a successful professional - says she owes all that she has become to her mother; her middle child wanted no-one else but his Mum when he was sick in hospital recently.

What are your first impressions of Karen?_____
_____

Would you like Karen if you met her? Why?/Why not?_____
_____

Sheila's daughter is a very successful lawyer. She is a high achiever who received top marks and awards at her University. She is also an accomplished horse rider who has met and ridden with some of Melbourne's most elite families, some of whom ride each year with the Royal Family. She enjoys buying designer clothes and collecting designer handbags and shoes. Sheila is a proud mother and likes to tell others about her daughter's success.

What are your first impressions of Sheila?_____

_____

Would you like Sheila if you met her? Why?/Why not?_____

_____

Louise is a very honest person who has always been concerned about others and tries to do what she can about the injustices in the world. Sometimes this gets her into trouble with her employers and the authorities because she speaks her mind if she thinks someone is being treated unfairly. Even her family wish she would keep quiet sometimes.

What are your first impressions of Louise? _____

_____

Would you like Louise if you met her?_____

_____

So, now you have had a brief introduction to the lives of these women and made judgements about them. Each of these vignettes highlights a particular story for each of these women. It is important to remember that our lives are multi-storied and no one story is going to tell you about the full richness of a person's life. When we meet someone we tend to give a quick summary of who we are based on what seems to be most dominant in our lives at that particular time. Similarly, people introducing themselves to us will give us a snap-shot of their lives in a few sentences. We cannot know all about their joys and disappointments, their successes and failures, their fears and hopes.

I can now reveal to you that the stories from these six women are in fact the multiple stories from **one person's** life. One person, who at various times in their life has felt confident or lacking in self-esteem, positive and happy, or sad and depressed. The question of where this person is in their life, and whether they are connected to positive or not-so-positive aspects of it, will determine which story they will choose to share and which story will be the dominant one. It may be the problem-saturated stories, or it may be the more competent stories and sparkling moments. Some of these stories may no longer reflect the life of the story-teller.

Perhaps she has changed and moved away from some of these earlier stories, but these stories never completely disappear from our lives, they just have less impact.

Sometimes the problem-saturated stories can return to haunt us when we experience disappointment, pain or loss. Then they can become less accessible when things are going well for us. Would you judge these aspects of the one person differently now you know that they are the sum of all these things; or at least they have been at some stage in their life?

When I do this exercise in groups, the participants are taken by surprise and often feel guilty that they have been too quick to judge and called Sheila a snob, or Ruth a know-it-all, or that Sarah and Jenny need to 'toughen up'. We all do that. As I said, our brains are designed to survey, assess and categorise and put things into cognitive boxes quickly – a little like computer files. But we need to give people the benefit of the doubt. We need to suspend judgement, particularly when we are challenged by people who are difficult and press our buttons. Maybe a story exists that we are unaware of that would change our perspective.

I learnt this myself when I was working on a research project with a woman who was extremely demanding. It seemed there was nothing I could do that was good enough. This woman, who was the project leader, was very intelligent, strong, and a little intimidating - tall with short dark hair and a solid build. Her social skills were seriously lacking – she never wasted time on simple courtesies and she came across to many who worked with her as aggressive. We were working to a very tight deadline for a government project and she pushed and pushed until one day I thought I couldn't take it any more. One of the department's staff realised I was stressed and upset and came to see what the problem was. I told her I was finding my boss's demands and lack of consideration difficult to manage. The staff member empathised and then told me about the woman's early life.

Apparently she had been orphaned at age five when both her parents were killed in a car accident. She was then raised by an aunt who didn't want or particularly like children. The aunt met the child's basic and physical needs, but there was very little interaction between them and the child spent a lot of time alone and in her room. I was so saddened by this story that it completely changed my feelings about this woman. From that day, nothing this woman could do would upset me. I understood the context of her lack of social skills and no longer took it personally and I finished the project on time. The supervisor hadn't changed, the circumstances of the project hadn't changed, I hadn't changed. But my perspective – the way I thought about the situation – had changed. Now, whenever I am confronted by someone else's challenging behaviour, instead of reacting to it, I think to myself, 'I wonder what has happened in this person's life to make them this way?'

Whether we like or accept the fact, others will judge us from the stories we tell about ourselves. I was raised to not judge others and I never really understood that others did make judgements until quite recently in my life. It had never occurred to me that I was being judged by others on the basis of what school I went to, what my father's occupation was, where I lived, what car I drove, what job I had and, more recently, which university I went to. I didn't realise that when I kept telling others about the problem stories in my life, they were hearing stories of failure and distancing from someone who was full of bad luck and negativity, while I thought I was telling stories of survival and resilience. In any event, I was continuing to give energy to aspects of my life that I didn't want and I needed to start telling the story of the life that I DID want.

This doesn't mean by the way, that we reject those problem stories. They are the stories of our lives and they have helped us to move forward by providing contrast between what we want and what we don't want. As with everyone else's lives, my life is multi-storied and some stories are problem-stories and some stories are success and competence stories.

I deliberately focus more now on telling the stories that fit with what I want for my life and have largely stopped telling the stories of unhappiness, disappointment, struggle, and pain, even though I know they are still there under the surface and can occasionally be re-triggered. Sometimes I will deliberately choose to share one of those stories with a client, so that they can see that it is possible to move from problem stories to alternative happier stories and have a sense of hope that things can be different for them.

So, STOP telling the negative problem stories of your life. And STOP engaging with others who want you to tell this story. Sometimes that includes counsellors, or other depressed or negative people.

A 2008 study concluded that extensive discussions of problems and encouragement of 'problem talk,' rehashing the details of problems, speculating about problems, and dwelling on negative emotions in particular, leads to a significant increase in the stress hormone cortisol, which in turn predicts **increased** depression and anxiety over time.[1] As you now know, this negativity is being 'passed on' through mirror genes to others around you – no wonder there is an epidemic of mood disorders.

So, start telling stories that are more in line with the life you would want to have – actively look for 'sparkling moments' or 'unique outcomes' – events that stand in contrast to the dominant or problem story. They will be there, but you might have to go on an archaeological dig to find them. Then look for even more events that support this alternative story and spend time with others who can support this view of your life and make this story richer. Tell this positive story more often and the impact or influence of the problem story will diminish in a similar way to the grooves on a record or CD that we talked about in relation to laying down new neural pathways. Trust me. I have seen it many times in my clinical work and personally, since I stopped talking about all the difficulties I have survived, my life is much more positive. I have fewer disappointments and am better at handling them when they do come into my life.

I remain focussed as much as I possibly can on what I do want, rather than what I don't want in my life, and keep bringing myself back to this whenever I have wandered off into negativity.

We have a choice about which story we would prefer to be experiencing and sharing with others – that's the story we need to tell more often.

I hope the Women's Stories exercise encourages you to withhold judgement and practise compassion when you next meet someone, even if they seem a little disagreeable. I would want others to do that for me. You see, the stories of Jenny, Ruth, Sarah, Karen, Sheila and Louise – they are actually stories from MY life.

(Endnotes)
1. Byrd-Craven, J., Geary, D. C., Rose, A. J., & Ponzi, D. (2008). "Co-ruminating increase stress hormone levels in women," Hormones and Behavior, 53, 489–492.

Chapter 8 – The Importance of Values

Why are values important? Because they are our guiding principles. We wouldn't start out on a long road journey without maps and we cannot successfully navigate our lives without guiding principles. How are we to measure whether we are living our lives well? Values give us the standards to which we hold ourselves to account and to measure the achievements of our lives.

In the past, our values were likely to have been handed down to us by our grand-parents, parents, or religious and civic leaders. But with the decline of religion in recent years, family break-down, and the expansion of global capitalism and consumerism, many people now feel disconnected from values that would give their lives direction and meaning. This disconnection from values is being experienced across cultures. I met recently with a group of Aboriginal Elders, who were telling me about their acute concerns that their young people seem to have lost their way; that they are living without traditional respect for their Elders, their families, the land and their culture, and that this was leading to significant levels of psychological and physical illness and family breakdown within young Indigenous families, as well as loss of traditional custom and practice and language. These Elders were of the firm view that they needed to engage with their young people around values and culture and that this would need to start at the earliest possible age – definitely pre-school.

As outlined in Chapter One, the values of consumerism and individualism of the last few decades seem to have failed to contribute anything positive to our identities and sense of purpose or meaning. I believe it can be a source of stress for us to live in a world that reflects back values that are inconsistent with our own, leading to alienation and, potentially, depression. For example, it seems that some companies within the telecommunications industry, deliberately make their service contracts so confusing that the consumer cannot compare services and prices with those offered by other providers. Because of this many people have been caught out by the small print in contracts that are complex and many pages long. Some services are included in our plan and some are not, but often we won't know until we get our bill. Similarly, some food producers have reduced the size of their products without informing the consumer yet continue charging the same price for less. Some products have been deliberately manipulated to be more cost effective for the producer, but significantly lower in quality for the consumer. For example, it recently came to light that some butchers in Australia were creating an apparently expensive cut of steak by using a glue to form cheaper meat into a product that looked more like the expensive option. The meat glue, a white powder known as transglutaminase, was sprinkled over small pieces of inferior quality meat, mixed and bound together to form a single piece of meat, wrapped in plastic wrap and refrigerated overnight. The result was a log of meat that could be carved into what looked deceptively like expensive fillet steaks.[1]

These unethical actions reflect attitudes of disrespect, dishonesty and an individualistic need to prosper at the expense of others. When these lack of values come into conflict with our own values, it causes dissonance or dis-ease within us, which I believe can impact upon our health. Since these practices seem to have become more and more commonplace, we often can't or don't express our feelings about it. But we do feel it – and it manifests as stress and anxiety in response to feeling a lack of certainty, a lack of trust, a lack of feeling valued, a lack of safety within our environment and a sense of powerlessness. I know for myself, when I hear of these practices, I feel dis-ease. I feel upset that someone would knowingly and deliberately treat me and others so contemptuously in the pursuit of maximising their profits, since my personal values reflect the Golden Rule 'Do unto others as you would have done unto you'.

So, in the absence of corporate, civic, religious or even familial leadership, how are we to identify the values that lead to us living our lives well? Well, we develop our sense of what is right or wrong from a number of sources, including from our parents and other key adults who may have influenced us as we were growing up, for example, grandparents, teachers, sports coaches, etc.

But we also develop our values from our own life experiences and from experiences where what we value may have been *absent*. For example, my father grew up in a family with an abusive father and witnessed violent assaults against his mother. My father is the most passive, gentle man, who values non-violence, tolerance and acceptance.

As we become adults ourselves, we often choose whether to maintain or reject the values we experienced as we were growing up based on our own unique experiences and beliefs.

The Importance of Values

Whilst some values may seem universal, others are culturally derived and may change with the times. For example, a generation ago many women may have been valued for qualities that were consistent with their roles as mothers and wives such as nurturance, affection, tradition, cleanliness etc. But today Australian women's values tend to reflect their economic independence and increasing participation in the workforce, although they may retain some of the more traditional values associated with being wives and mothers. Nor is ethical living the same as living according to certain morals. Some groups within our society may develop moral standards that are not necessarily seen as ethical by all citizens. For example, some churches' views on homosexuality, pre-marital sex and contraception. These things are no longer prohibited through our legal and judicial systems, reflecting that the broader society view is different to that of the religious sector.

In a wonderful book titled *Tuesdays With Morrie*, a university professor (Morrie), who is writing about his life as it comes to an end, has this to say about our values: 'Here's what I mean by building your own sub-culture. I don't mean you disregard every rule of your community. I don't go around naked, for example. I don't run through red lights. The little things, I can obey. But the big things – how we think, what we value – those you must choose for yourself. You can't let anyone – or any society – determine those for you.'[2]

So let's now try to get clear about the values that may be guiding your life, or that you would like to guide your life.

Have a look at the list of values on the following pages. I know it is a large list and might look a little daunting, but I wanted to make sure that I captured as many values that had relevance across as many cultures that contribute to contemporary Australian society as I could. Some may seem strange values to you, but they may have relevance for someone else.

Step 1: Look through the complete list of values and with a highlighter pen if you have one, highlight those values that you feel are important to you, or resonate with you. If you don't have a highlighter underline or circle them.

Step 2: Now from the list of values that you have highlighted or circled, I want you to reduce this list down to no more than ten values. These should be the values that you could not imagine living your life without. Keep this list of ten values as one that you can reflect on again.

Step 3: From the ten values you have highlighted, I now want you to identify your Top Three Values and…

Step 4: Using the worksheet that follows the List of Values, for each one of Your Top Three Values, I want you to answer the following three questions:-

1. What did I learn about this value growing up?

Was this value present or absent in your family of origin? Why was it important within your family? How was this value given expression – or if it was absent, what impact did its absence have on your family?

EXAMPLE:

I value HONESTY. I learnt when I was growing up that this was an important value for my parents and they wanted me to carry it on. I was punished more harshly for lying than for owning up to my mistakes. We were always encouraged to tell the truth, no matter what. I value honesty myself as an adult, because it allows me to trust the people in my life. I have encouraged my children to carry on this value.

---

2. Why is this value important to me?

How is my life improved when this value is present? Do my current life circumstances allow me to live consistently with this value? Are there people or situations around me that consistently violate this value? What would need to change?

EXAMPLE:

This value is important to me, because I believe that honesty is the foundation of positive relationships. I cannot have close relationships with people I cannot trust. This value is currently present in my personal life in the way I want it to be. All of my key relationships are with people I can trust because they value honesty also.

It upsets me when the corporate world tries to deceive us. I would like the corporate world to hold itself to more ethical, honest business practices.

3. **If I was living my life the way I want to, how would this value be expressed?**

   What would my life look like if this value was present in my life the way I want it to be?

EXAMPLE:

I will be in a close relationship with someone who is always honest with me and I would have friends who value honesty. I would work for an employer who conducts honest, ethical trading. I would do business with people who value honesty in their transactions with me and others.

VALUES LIST

Abundance	Autonomy	Charm
Acceptance	Awe	Cheerfulness
Accomplishment	Balance	Clarity
Accountability	Beauty	Cleanliness
Accuracy	Belonging	Closeness
Achievement	Benevolence	Collaboration
Adaptability	Bliss	Commitment
Adventure	Boldness	Communication
Aestheticism	Bravery	Community
Affection	Brilliance	Compassion
Altruism	Calmness	Competence
Ambition	Capability	Competition
Appreciation	Caring	Confidence
Assertiveness	Carefulness	Connection
Attentiveness	Celebrity	Consciousness
Attractiveness	Certainty	Consistency
Audacity	Challenge	Contentment
Authority	Change	Continuity

Contribution	Empathy	Focus
Control	Encouragement	Forgiveness
Conviction	Endurance	Fortitude
Co-operation	Energy	Freedom
Cordiality	Enjoyment	Friendship
Courage	Entertainment	Frugality
Courtesy	Enthusiasm	Fun
Creativity	Equality	Gallantry
Credibility	Excellence	Generosity
Curiosity	Excitement	Genuineness
Daring	Exhilaration	Giving
Decisiveness	Expediency	God's Will
Delight	Experience	Goodness
Democracy	Expertise	Grace
Dependability	Exploration	Gratitude
Depth	Extroversion	Growth
Determination	Exuberance	Guidance
Devotion	Fairness	Happiness
Dignity	Faith	Hard work
Diligence	Faithfulness	Harmony
Directness	Fame	Health
Discipline	Family	Helpfulness
Discovery	Fashion	Heroism
Discretion	Fearlessness	Holiness
Diversity	Ferocity	Honesty
Dominance	Fidelity	Honour
Drive	Fierceness	Hopefulness
Duty	Financial security	Humility
Ecology	Fitness	Humour
Education	Flair	Imagination
Effectiveness	Flexibility	Impact
Efficiency	Flow	Impartiality
Elegance	Fluency	Independence

The Importance of Values

Industry	Merit	Precision
Inner peace	Mindfulness	Privacy
Innovation	Modesty	Professionalism
Insightfulness	Motivation	Prosperity
Inspiration	Mystery	Prudence
Integrity	Nature	Punctuality
Intelligence	Neatness	Purity
Intensity	Nerve	Purpose
Intimacy	Non-conformity	Realism
Introversion	Non-violence	Reason
Intuition	Nurturance	Recreation
Inventiveness	Obedience	Refinement
Joy	Open-mindedness	Relaxation
Justice	Openness	Reliability
Kindness	Optimism	Religiousness
Kinship	Order	Resilience
Knowledge	Originality	Resolve
Land connection	Passion	Resourcefulness
Leadership	Patience	Respect
Learning	Peace	Responsibility
Leisure	Perceptiveness	Responsiveness
Liberty	Perfection	Restraint
Liveliness	Perseverance	Reverence
Logic	Persistence	Richness
Longevity	Personal growth	Risk
Looking good	Persuasiveness	Ritual
Lore	Philanthropy	Sacredness
Love	Playfulness	Safety
Loyalty	Pleasure	Satisfaction
Mastery	Poise	Security
Maturity	Popularity	Self-acceptance
Meekness	Power	Self-esteem
Meaning	Practicality	Self-control

Self-knowledge
Selflessness
Self-reliance
Sensitivity
Sensuality
Serenity
Service
Sexuality
Sharing
Significance
Silence
Silliness
Simplicity
Sincerity
Skillfulness
Solidarity
Solitude
Speed
Spirituality
Spontaneity
Stability
Status
Strength
Structure
Success
Support
Surprise
Sympathy
Temperance
Thankfulness
Thoroughness
Thoughtfulness
Thrift

Tidiness
Tolerance
Tradition
Tranquility
Transcendence
Trust
Truth
Understanding
Uniqueness
Unity
Usefulness
Utility
Valor
Variety
Virtue
Vision
Vitality
Warmth
Wealth
Wisdom
Wit
Wonder
World Peace
Youthfulness
Zest

My Primary Values

My Top Ten Values:-

1. _____ 6. _____
2. _____ 7. _____
3. _____ 8. _____
4. _____ 9. _____
5. _____ 10. _____

My Essential Three Values:-

1. _____ 2. _____
3. _____

What did I learn about this value growing up? Was this value present or absent in my childhood?

Value 1. _____
_____
_____

Value 2. _____
_____
_____

Value 3. _____
_____
_____

Why is this value important to me?

Value 1. _____

_____

_____

Value 2. _____

_____

_____

Value 3. _____

_____

_____

If I was living my life the way I want to, how would this value be expressed?

Value 1. _____

_____

_____

Value 2. _____

_____

_____

Value 3. _____

_____

_____

The Importance of Values

You have now identified your primary values and how your life would look if they were more present in your life. In the next chapter you will be identifying your Character Strengths.

If you are able to give full expression to your values and strengths, you will begin to live with a sense of greater purpose and meaningfulness.

(Endnotes)
1. Mail Online, 15 May, 2012. www.dailymail.co.uk
2. Ablom, Mitch. *Tuesdays with Morrie.* (USA: Broadway Books, 2002).

Chapter 9 – Identify Your Character Strengths

Just as values act as guidelines for us to live our lives well and with personal integrity, knowing our strengths help us to match our desires for our lives with our innate abilities and aptitudes.

> Character cannot be developed in ease and quiet. Only through experience of trial and suffering can the soul be strengthened, ambition inspired, and success achieved.
>
> *Helen Keller*

You will recall that in Chapter Two, I outlined the work of Dr Martin Seligman and introduced you to his Six Core Virtues and Twenty-four Character Strengths. Dr Seligman has made it possible for you to take the VIA Signature Strengths Survey for free online at www.authentichappiness.org

If you are not connected to the internet, you can take the test by getting a copy of Dr Seligman's book *Authentic Happiness* from a bookstore or library. The online test will rate your strengths in order and give you a summary of your top five strengths and their meanings. These five top signature strengths are the ones that you will need to pay attention to in order to assess whether you are currently using them, and if not, what you may be able to do to take advantage of them more often. Once you have taken the test, have a look at your top scoring strength and ask yourself these questions:-

- In the life that I am living now, am I able to give sufficient expression to this number one strength?
- If not, what would I need to change?

Repeat these two questions for each of the top five primary strengths.

I took Dr Seligman's survey myself in 2010, at a time when I was feeling a little stuck and dissatisfied – particularly in my professional life – and even contemplating whether to leave the profession of psychology. The results of taking the online survey identified my top five strengths as follows:-

1. Judgement, critical thinking and open-mindedness
2. Curiosity and interest in the world
3. Honesty, authenticity and genuineness
4. Bravery and valour

5. Creativity, ingenuity, and originality

At this time, I was working very long hours in clinical consultation, mostly from one private practice clinic, whilst also doing two Aboriginal health clinics each week. The work was largely repetitive and had become somewhat routine and unchallenging for me. (I don't want to seem disrespectful of my clients when I say this. It was nothing to do with them or their stories. I like to think that my waning energy for clinical work did not show to them during their sessions and my professional approach to my work endured.) Nevertheless, when I answered the two questions for each of my strengths, it became clear to me that Strength No 2 and Strength No 5 did not have adequate opportunity for expression in my life.

When I gave this some thought, I remembered how much I used to write. It has been something I have enjoyed since childhood. I also enjoyed being creative in other ways including art, sewing, developing projects, writing workshops, cooking, and craftwork. As a result of this awareness, I began to think about starting the research (Strength No 2) towards writing a book (Strength No 5). Although I continued to work in clinical practice, I felt invigorated by having begun the process that would permit me to use these two innate strengths, which I had allowed to become stifled by other demands. Both my clinical work and I were re-energised and sustained whilst work began on this book.

I hope that once you have answered the two questions for each of your top five strengths, you will have some ideas for giving greater expression to those strengths that you have identified as lacking.

If you should have any difficulty here, there are a number of books, mostly based on personality theory, which can give suggestions for types of work or activity that are a good match for a particular personality strength. Some are listed within the Suggested Reading guide at the end of the book.

Identify Your Character Strengths

The Future I Am Creating

How can I bring my Values and my Strengths together in order to be living my life more meaningfully?

My Top Three Values   My Top Three Strengths
1. _____   1. _____
2. _____   2. _____
3. _____   3. _____

Chapter 10 – Set Intentions and Goals

'He has achieved success who has lived well, laughed often and loved much; who has enjoyed the trust and love of good people; who has filled his niche and accomplished his task; who has left the world a better place.'

Bessie A Stanley

So, returning for a moment to what the research tells us about happiness, if we accept the broader definition of sustainable happiness as meaning and purpose, we need to make a contribution, we need to be active. We are happiest when we are achieving. Aristotle believed that happiness was everyone's ultimate goal, but that it didn't always come easily. Just as 'One swallow does not a summer make', one pleasant day does not make a happy life, and he went on to call happiness an 'activity' that required skill, focus and active effort. Schoch agrees, 'Far from being a state of passive enjoyment, like relaxing in a bubble bath or eating a box of chocolates, happiness demands active effort. Being happy, then is something that we resolve to achieve rather than something pleasant that comes our way like sunshine after a rainstorm.'[1]

Martin Seligman too, in revising his authentic happiness theory into wellbeing theory acknowledges the importance of achievement or accomplishment for its own sake. The research into the factors that contribute to our happiness generally indicate that a sense of achievement makes us happy. Our minds and bodies are designed to be forward moving and we are happier when we are – hence depressed people often have difficulty with activity and movement.

Goals are important tools for keeping us focussed on what we *Do* want. I find it useful to set small goals each month. On each first day of the month, in the same diary that I use for recording my five positive statements of gratitude each day, I set myself between three and five small goals.

FOR EXAMPLE – MY MONTHLY GOALS IN FEBRUARY, 2011 were:

1.	Clean out my wardrobe
2.	Go swimming three times a week
3.	Book out two weeks for a holiday in July
4.	Write script for relaxation CD

At the end of each month, I go back to the first day and review my goals and mark off which ones I have achieved and decide whether to carry through to the next month those that I have not accomplished. Sometimes our goals will change and we may decide not to carry them through. That's OK – there is no right or wrong way. It is just important that the goals we are setting are in line with the vision of where we want to be. Even if we achieve only half of our stated goals, that's over twenty goals achieved each year.

Des Renford, Australia's greatest marathon swimmer, who swam the English Channel no fewer than nineteen times, said when interviewed about his success: 'God has been pretty good to us. He gave us fourteen billion brain cells and he gave us an imagination as well. If you can see yourself obtaining your goal then that picture is going to contribute immeasurably towards your success. You cannot compete or perform in a manner which is inconsistent to how you see yourself.' You may be able to see the techniques that Des is drawing on here in those we have identified in earlier chapters:

- State an Intention
- Visualise and Affirm it
- Mentally Rehearse it
- Focus on what you *Do* want, not on what you *Don't* want

So let's return for a moment to the exercise you did in Chapter Six when you identified what your Ideal Life would look like.

Enter that vision into the next exercise sheet headed *Goal Setting and Motivation*. This is designed to get you thinking about how you can start being active and moving yourself ever closer towards the achievement of that preferred image of your life.

Remember it is important to acknowledge every effort, not just the achievement. Whenever you experience a setback re-focus your attention on what you *do* want, rather than on what you don't want, and don't lose faith that what you want is achievable.

As many successful people will attest, there is only one difference between someone who successfully achieves their goals and someone who doesn't - and that is PERSEVERANCE. Never, never give up. Bryce Courtenay, a prolific and successful author with dual South African and Australian citizenship, began writing at age 55 after ending his career as a 'drunken executive', giving up his one hundred-cigarette-a-day habit, his drinking habit and losing eighteen kilograms. He describes the experience of becoming a writer as opening his 'dream tank'. 'Think of an oil refinery standing in the desert lit up in the dark –

the human brain is like that.' The oil refinery carries major tanks or potential talents that each of us is born with, but, 'Most of us don't turn the major tap on because we are so shit scared of life, so terrified of the gush that might follow that we find the smallest little tank and tell ourselves we're happy with the drips we milk from it.'[2]

Three Keys to Personal Success:	
Believe in Yourself	Self Esteem
Know Where You Want To Go	Vision, Goal-setting
Persistence – Don't Give Up	Motivation

Nelson Mandela, South African anti-apartheid revolutionary and former President of South Africa shared similar sentiments to Bryce Courtenay's when he said:

'There is no passion to be found playing small – in settling for a life that is less than the one you are capable of living.'

The following quote entitled 'Fear' has been wrongly attributed to Nelson Mandela's Inaugural Speech of 1994, but it is in fact a quote from author Marianne Williamson from her book *A Return to Love: Reflections on the Principles of A Course in Miracles*. Harper Collins, USA, 1992.

Fear

Our deepest fear is not that we are inadequate.

Our deepest fear is that we are powerful beyond measure.

It is our light, not our darkness that frightens us.

We ask ourselves, who am I to be brilliant, gorgeous, talented and fabulous?

Actually who are you *not* to be?

You are a child of God.

Your playing small doesn't serve the world.

> There's nothing enlightened about shrinking so that other people won't feel insecure around you.
>
> We are all meant to shine, as children do.
>
> We were born to make manifest the glory of God that is within us.
>
> It's not just in some of us: It's in everyone.
>
> As we let our light shine, we unconsciously give other people permission to do the same.
>
> As we are liberated from our own fear, our presence automatically liberates others.
>
> *Marianne Williamson*

So, I invite you to let go of fear and embrace your power, or in the words of a song, 'Let your little light shine' and believe that you have unique skills, talents, abilities, and character strengths that are waiting for you to give expression to and to share with the world.

Key points to remember:-.

- Believe that what you want is possible.
- Affirm, Visualise, Imagine and Rehearse – OFTEN
- Review your goals from time to time to check that they are still in accord with what you DO want in your life
- Celebrate both effort and achievement
- Don't allow others or internal negative voices to undermine you
- Imagine regularly how it FEELS to be living your ideal life
- There are no mistakes – just learning experiences
- Never give up and Never beat yourself up
- Appreciate all that you have now

Goal Setting and Motivation

Ask yourself what you really want in life. In your Ideal World – where are you living? What are you doing? Are there others with you? If all your dreams in life were to come true, what would your life look like?

My dream:

_____

_____

_____

_____

_____

Now, if you are serious about getting there, what steps do you need to take? Think about these steps as moving you gradually but ever closer to your Ideal World.

What can I do today?

_____

_____

_____

What might I need to do over the next few months?

_____

_____

_____

What would I like to achieve in the next 12 months?

_____

_____

_____

Can I identify anyone who may be able to assist me in moving towards my goals?

_____

_____

_____

What barriers can I see between me and my goals? Tick the ones that you have the power to change, and think about what you might need to do to overcome these.

_____

_____

_____

(Endnotes)
1. Schoch, R. *The Secrets of Happiness – Three Thousand Years of Searching for the Good Life.* (USA:Scribner, 2006).
2. Bryce Courtenay in conversation with journalist Eve Lamb, Hamilton Spectator, April 16, 1994.

Chapter 11 – Maintain a Healthy Mind and Body

Much of this book so far has been about methods for relieving suffering of the mind and improving our mental state. However, mind and body are intricately linked and it is not possible to have good health for one without the other. Earlier I outlined some alarming trends over the past fifty years in relation to soil degradation, the increased use of chemical pesticides and herbicides, the increase in atmospheric and water pollutants and the increasing chemical alteration of our food – all of which I believe has contributed to unprecedented levels of chronic disease, including mental illness.

The Industrialisation of Our Food

Recent research continues to show that our food is half as nutritious as it was two generations ago. A study conducted by the University of Colorado, noted that the nutrient density of our food has declined approximately forty to sixty per cent since the early 1900s and is now lacking in the many vitally important vitamins, minerals, and trace elements that are essential for maintaining good health. This study found that compared with our grandparents, who ate an average of 59.4 kg per year of home-grown vegetables, we are eating only 4.9 kg. Comparing the levels of minerals in fruits and vegetables from 1963 with 1992, United States Department of Agriculture (USDA) figures showed:-

Mineral	Decline (Average %)
Magnesium	-21.08
Calcium	-29.82
Iron	-32.00
Phosphorous	-11.09
Potassium	- 6.48

The old adage 'An apple a day keeps the doctor away' now seems an improbable expectation, given that compared to the apple of 1914, today's apple has lost:

- 82% of its magnesium content
- 84% of its phosphorus
- 96% of its iron, and
- 48% of its calcium

In addition to the impact of soil depletion, the extensive use of chemicals in both food production and processing has led to many of our staple foods being structurally altered in ways that now make them toxic when we digest them.

Some of the most toxic foods are staples within the western diet and are foods that are amongst the first to be introduced to our babies, for example wheat. Wheat is an ancient food crop having first been cultivated over 10,000 years ago. Over 30,000 varieties have been identified by botanists, but with the advent of modern farming the number currently sown for production worldwide has dramatically decreased to just a handful, which account for ninety per cent of the total wheat grown in the world. The wheat that is grown today bears little resemblance to the ancient varieties, or even to the wheat that our grandparents ate.

In the 1950s scientists began cross-breeding wheat to make it hardier, shorter and higher-yielding. Today's bread wheat has only existed in cultivation having come about through hybridisation.

When grown in healthy, fertile soil, whole wheat is rich in vitamin E and B complex, many minerals, including calcium and iron, as well as omega-3 fatty acids. However, as a result of contemporary farming and milling methods, which result in the destruction of many of wheat's nutrients, large numbers of people have now become intolerant or allergic to modern-day wheat and wheat products.

Gluten sensitivity has increased four-fold over the last forty years with approximately one in a hundred Australians thought to be affected, though many remain undiagnosed and 20 million Americans are now diagnosed with Celiac Disease.

In addition to the genetic changes to wheat, modern farming practices have led to ever-increasing use of pesticides, fungicides, and other chemicals designed to increase levels of production and yield. Even before the wheat seeds are sown into the soil, they receive applications of fungicides and pesticides, some of which are known to increase our susceptibility to neurotoxic disease and cancer. Many of the pesticides function as xenoestrogens, which disrupt our normal hormonal balance, leading some researchers to speculate that these chemicals may be contributing factors to puberty occurring at earlier ages, increases in breast cancer, endometriosis and fertility problems. After the crops are harvested, the grain is stored in bins and sprayed with up to six different insecticide chemicals, often on more than one occasion, since it can be in storage for up to a year. If random sampling identifies just one live insect per litre of grain, fumigation utilising highly toxic chemicals is undertaken. Then, in the grain drying process, heat damage can result in the denaturing of the protein. Denaturation results in the change in a protein's shape and consequent loss of its function brought about by heat, agitation, acid, alcohol, heavy metals or other agents.

High speed milling, where temperatures can reach 400 degrees Fahrenheit, destroys vital nutrients and creates rancidity. Vitamin E, which once used to be readily available from wheat, is destroyed in milling.

NUTRIENT LOSS FROM REFINING OF WHEAT[1]

Thiamine (B1) -77%	Riboflavin (B2) -80%
Niacin -81%	Pyridoxine (B6) -72%
Pantothenic acid -50%	Vitamin E -86%
Calcium -60%	Phosphorous -71%
Magnesium -84%	Potassium -77%
Sodium -78%	Chromium -40%
Manganese -86%	Iron -76%
Cobalt -89%	Zinc -78%
Copper -68%	Selenium -16%
Molybdenum -48%	

Dr William Davis, cardiologist and author of a book titled *Wheat Belly* believes that the new form of wheat produced by large-scale agri-business is toxic. Dr Davis advises that a protein within the wheat, gliadin (a part of gluten), is broken down when ingested in the gut into small polypeptides, which are small enough to penetrate into the brain and affect behaviour.

Dr Davis asserts that this can distort attention and activity in children, cause mania in those suffering bi-polar, paranoia and hallucinations in schizophrenics. Due to it degrading into a morphine-like compound after eating, it stimulates appetite causing cravings for more wheat.

Dr Davis says that there are now thousands of research papers, which have demonstrated the biochemical changes in the gluten protein as a result of modern large-scale farming practices and he believes that wheat consumption in the western world is contributing significantly to the current high levels of obesity. Wheat has a high glycaemic index (GI) and is more efficient at converting to blood sugar than just about any other carbohydrate, including sucrose! Glycaemic Index provides a measure of how quickly blood sugar levels rise after eating a particular type of food relative to pure glucose which has a GI of 100.

Dr Maria Alvarez, who specialises in nutritional programs for obese patients, has found in her practice over two decades that for every ten people with digestive disturbances, obesity, irritable bowel syndrome, diabetes, arthritis, and heart disease, eight out of the ten have a problem with wheat. Once removed from their diet, their symptoms generally disappear within three to six months. Dr Alvarez predicts that in a few years time as many as eighty per cent of people will stop eating wheat.

Given that wheat supplies about twenty per cent of the total food calories worldwide and has become a national staple in many countries, there is cause for concern. Apart from being used as breakfast cereals and in breads, wheat has been used as an additive to many other products including sauces and gravies. Americans eat an average of sixty-six kilograms of wheat per person per year and at the same time they are experiencing escalating rates of chronic inflammatory disease including diabetes, arthritis, and heart disease.

Before going on to have a look at what we can do positively to enhance good nutrition for healthy minds and bodies, let's take a look at another popular 'food' source – sugar - and how patterns of its use have changed over recent decades.

Sugar consumption has increased from just over eight kilograms per person per annum in 1800 to forty-one kilograms per person in 1900; and to a whopping eighty-one kilograms per person per annum, in 2009.

Put differently, sugar consumption has risen from four teaspoons per person per day in 1990 to twenty-two teaspoons today, and much of that is the result of increased consumption of soft drinks, which often contain as much as 15-18 teaspoons of sugar in an average size bottle. As with wheat, a lot of our sugar consumption is hidden by being incorporated into processed foods, including many deceptively labelled 'light', or 'low-fat', or 'all natural'.

In the 1980s when the prevailing evil in our diet was considered to be fat, many food manufacturers used sugar both as a preservative and an additive to improve the taste of low-fat foods. The impact of such dramatic increases in the consumption of sugar is evident in the many alarming chronic illness statistics, predominantly diabetes and obesity. In 1893 there were three cases of diabetes per 100,000 people and today that figure has risen to 8,000 per 100,000!

Australia is now ranked as one of the fattest countries in the developed world with over fourteen million Australians being overweight or obese; a doubling of prevalence in the last twenty years. Even more alarming, Indigenous Australians are twice as likely as non-Indigenous to become obese and currently have the fourth highest ranking of likelihood to suffer Type 2 diabetes in the world. Obesity has overtaken smoking as the leading cause of death and if current trends continue, it is expected that by 2025 close to eighty per cent of all adults and thirty per cent of children will be overweight or obese. These trends also predict that by the time they are age twenty, our current generation of children will, for the first time, have shorter life-expectancies than past generations. How have we arrived at this point?

We know that nutrients are vital for healthy cells and we now know about the role of epigenetics and how environmental stressors including our diet, our exposure to toxins and our exposure to stress or trauma can alter our own gene expression and have an impact through our children and grandchildren for several generations.

Why is This Happening?
In a word – money!

There have been significant changes to the food that we eat over the past fifty to one hundred years, which has completely compromised its nutritional content in the name of making big profits for primary producers, chemical fertiliser companies and food manufacturers. Similarly some large pharmaceutical companies have at times been found to have compromised professional, ethical and scientific research in the name of continuing sales of harmful products in the name of making mega-profits.

Nutritional information about the types of foods or nutrients that we need to be healthy and the recommended daily intakes of these is generally assessed and reported by governments. However, both the food and pharmaceutical industries have powerful lobby groups and go to great lengths to protect their vested interest, including by nominating its own representatives to sit on government advisory panels, and by funding so called 'independent' research and by making available its own research, some of which has been manipulated to demonstrate benefit when it cannot be scientifically validated.

In 2009 for example, the Food and Drug Administration (FDA) admitted that four congressmen and its own former commissioner had unduly influenced a process that lead to the approval of a product for injured knees. Although FDA staff had unanimously found the device to be unsafe, their decision was subsequently over-turned. The manufacturer of the product coincidentally had made significant campaign contributions to all four congressmen.

The FDA is responsible in the United States for regulating all prescription and over the counter medications; medical devices such as heart valves and stents, and food and blood supply and yet due to budgetary constraints, the agency is forced to rely on funding from sources with private interests and financial motivations, rather than safeguarding consumers' health.

In fact, in 2009 it was reported that nearly all the FDA's budgetary increases over the previous five years had come from pharmaceutical companies, not government.

At the time of writing, a large European pharmaceutical company is under investigation in Japan after two Japanese universities found evidence of manipulation of clinical trial data, which they claim exaggerated the benefit of a blood pressure medication. The matter is under investigation by the Japanese Ministry of Health. And in February 2014 the Australian Assistant Health Minister became embroiled in controversy when it was revealed that her chief-of-staff had strong links to the food industry. He was co-owner of a company that had represented the food industry and previously worked as a lobbyist for several large food producers. The controversy emerged after the Assistant Minister intervened to shut down a website which was launching a new health-star-rating food labelling initiative. It came to light that her chief-of-staff had opposed a new front-of-pack labelling system for Australian foods on behalf of several major food companies he had previously represented as an industry lobbyist.[2]

Researchers who come to hold views that are in conflict with powerful industry and lobby groups are openly attacked and discredited, for example, Dr Andrew Wakefield of Austin, Texas, who has been investigating the links between stomach disorders and autism and the link with the Measles, Mumps, Rubella vaccine since 1996. As a result of his investigations and the publishing of his research in 1998, Dr Wakefield became the victim of a world-wide smear campaign that lead to him being persecuted to such an extent that he has been legally unable to practice medicine.

However, in recent months, pharmaceutical companies, governments and courts have quietly accepted the validity of Dr Wakefield's research and have paid out massive amounts of compensation to the victims, acknowledging the permanent damage to their health.

Autism is a childhood neurological disorder that disrupts normal childhood development and its rates have been rising dramatically. Speculation around the reason for such dramatic increase in prevalence has included the impact of vaccines, but also environmental and nutritional factors.

Rates of Autism	
1970:	1 in 10,000
1975:	1 in 5,000
1985:	1 in 2,500
2001:	1 in 250
2004:	1 in 166
2007:	1 in 150
2009:	1 in 110
2012:	1 in 88
2013:	1 in 50

Source: Whiteout Press

Such dramatic increases cannot simply be attributed to improved diagnosis and reporting.

I am not advocating the widespread abandoning of childhood immunisation. These vaccines have significantly reduced the incidence of exposure to severely debilitating diseases worldwide. But I am concerned about the lack of research into the long term effects of the toxic fillers within many vaccines and in the increasing number of vaccines that an infant is now exposed to within its first twelve months of life. In the 1950s children routinely received three vaccinations. Australian infants today will have received twenty-two vaccinations by the time of their first birthday.

Similarly, rates of asthma have also been steadily increasing in a number of countries. In the United States, for all age, sex, and racial groups there has been an overall seventy-five per cent increase in prevalence between 1980 and 1994.

Asthma prevalence increased 160 percent among children up to four years of age, where it is now the second highest prevalence behind children aged five to fourteen years. Based on figures from 2007-8, ten per cent of the Australian population have been identified as having asthma and amongst the Indigenous community asthma is the second most common self-reported illness.

Data from the US Centre for Disease Control (CDC) show that the average American child aged between six and eleven years carries unacceptable levels of the organophosphorus pesticides, chlorpyrifos and methyl parathion, both of which are known neurotoxins.

Statistics from both the United States and the United Kingdom indicate a rise in childhood leukaemia and brain cancer over the past twenty years, with many researchers identifying exposure to chemicals as a contributing factor.

Dr Richard Clapp, professor emeritus of environmental health at Boston University School of Public Health, claims that a portion of childhood cancers can be traced back to damage done at the cellular level from chemicals that are carcinogens, for example, chlorinated solvents commonly used in many household products.

If you have teenagers, you may be concerned by evidence from a recent Swedish study on the use of wireless phones, including mobiles and cordless phones, which has shown a link between electromagnetic radiation exposure and the risk of malignant and non-malignant brain tumours. This study reveals that those who used mobile or cordless phones for more than a year had a seventy per cent greater risk of developing brain cancer compared to those who used them for less than a year and in long term users (more than twenty-five years use) a three hundred percent risk of brain cancer.

This study supports an earlier decade-long thirteen-nation Interphone study, which found a 180 percent risk of brain cancer among those who used mobile phones for more than 1,640 hours in their lifetime. [3] In spite of the research findings, little has been done to provide improved protective standards for minimising the effects of exposure.

I could go on with more stories of how our food and environment has changed and with it our rates of chronic illness, but it is well documented already and I encourage you to seek the facts for yourself. There are several good websites these days that publish well researched, scientific data in relation to nutrition and pharmaceutical intervention.

It is my intention in this book to attempt to re-empower you with regards to the management of your health – physical, psychological and spiritual. Western medicine has made enormous gains over the past one hundred years and makes a valued contribution to the health of its citizens, notably in the fields of emergency medicine and surgery.

But there have also been some losses, I feel, and perhaps it is time for the pendulum to swing back towards medicine as healing, not just medicine as quick-fix drug intervention. It is clear that there are some very worrying trends, but we can become informed and take action.

Integrative Medicine

It is pleasing to note the increasing interest and practice in 'integrated' health care – which is medicine that combines the best of Western, scientific medicine with alternative or complementary therapies, which involve patients in their own healing. Both sectors have practitioners with enormous knowledge and skill which, when combined, is formidable and gives the patient the 'best of both worlds' in their treatment options. As early as the 1990s in the natural medicine industry we were saying that it was not fat but sugar that was contributing more to obesity and chronic illness, and that there was a difference between 'good' fats and 'bad' fats. We were not generally listened to by medical practitioners, many of whom continued to advise their patients not to eat eggs or avocadoes and to disregard the advice (often labelled 'quackery') of complementary or alternative medicine (CAM) practitioners.

Many doctors now have an understanding of the difference in fats and the role of glycaemic index (GI) in affecting metabolism.

Similarly, I recall advising my patients with inflammation to use fish oils (omega-3) long before they were in general use, and being criticised by some doctors, who refused to believe the robust research that had been conducted and published by reputable natural medicine companies.

In the meantime, patients who were consulting with naturopaths and following a low-GI diet rather than a low fat diet were losing weight, recovering from inflammatory diseases, and improving their health outcomes.

Omega-3:Omega-6 Imbalance

The dietary intake of omega-3 fatty acids has dramatically declined in Western countries over the last one hundred years and much of this is due once again to changes in our food. Omega-3 and omega-6 are known as essential fatty acids (EFAs), because although they are required by our body for good health, our bodies cannot make them – they must be supplied through our diet.

The ideal ratio of omega-3 to omega-6 essential fatty acids (EFAs) is approx. 1:1 but the North American diet currently has omega-6 fats outnumbering omega 3 fats by a ratio of 20:1, largely as a result of the adding of various omega-6 rich oils (corn, sunflower, safflower, cottonseed) directly to food or through animal feed.

Omega-3 EFAs are thought to be important not only with regards to inflammation, but for nervous system health and are essential for healthy brain functioning. Studies have consistently found that frequent fish consumption (oily fish is high in omega-3) is associated with decreased risk of depression, aggression and suicidal ideation. A number of investigations have found decreased levels of omega-3 content in the blood of depressed patients.

Studies involved in the introduction of omega-3s to prisoners in the United States and United Kingdom for example, found that violent behaviour was decreased by at least thirty per cent, compared with controls who did not receive supplementation.

The researchers involved in the prison trials, Joseph Hibbeln and his colleagues, also mapped the increase in omega-6 fatty acids from seed oils in thirty-eight countries since the 1960s and found that homicide rates went up in all countries over the same period in a linear progression. Interestingly, countries that eat large quantities of fish in their diet such as Japan have low rates of murder and depression. Of course, such studies can only demonstrate a correlation between omega-3 and aggressive behaviour – they cannot claim a causal relationship.

The same research team has investigated the effects of deficiencies in EFAs at times when the brain is growing, for example, whilst still in the mother's uterus, during the first five years of life and at puberty. The researchers report that animal studies have found that parents deprived of omega-3 over two generations produce offspring who are unable to release dopamine and serotonin effectively (neurotransmitters that are important for mood regulation, reward and digestion). 'The extension of all this is that if children are left with low dopamine as a result of early deficits in their own or their mother's diets, they cannot experience reward in the same way and they cannot learn from reward and punishment. If their serotonin levels are low, they cannot inhibit their impulses or regulate their emotional responses.'[4]

It seems to me that the researchers are perfectly describing much of what we see in clinic today, along with our paediatric colleagues, labelled as autism spectrum disorder, or attention-deficit-hyperactivity disorder, or oppositional defiant disorder – all of which have been increasing in prevalence in the Western world.

In the first study in the world to investigate the relationship between dietary habits of pregnant mothers and the influence that their diet has on the mental health of their children, Australian Associate Professor Felice Jacka, a psychiatric epidemiologist, has found startling results that will undoubtedly revolutionise our understanding of the relationship between diet and predisposition to mental illness.

The study which involved more than 23,000 mothers and children found that early life diet – including the nutrition received in-utero can cause anxiety, depression and behavioural problems in children. Dr Jacka has called on governments around the world to take immediate action to limit the low-nutrient junk food that has become so widely available and which is contributing to such poor mental health outcomes and growing rates of obesity for our children.[5]

The Brain-Gut Axis

Research in the field of nutritional and environmental medicine has identified a vital and two-way link between the gastro-intestinal tract, (called the Enteric Nervous System - ENS) the central nervous system (CNS) and the fight or flight system (the Autonomic Nervous System - ANS). This system has become known as the 'Brain-gut Axis'.

Research into this interactive system has been helpful to assist medical professionals in developing an understanding of the link between thoughts, emotions and physiological experiences.

This new evidence legitimises the 'mind-body connection' and begins to break down Western medicine's compartmentalisation of our bodies. Specialist areas of medicine continue to steadfastly focus on primarily one area or system, for example, psychiatry, gastroenterology, dietetics, without venturing into other systems with which their field of specialisation may interact, most notably between the mind and the body . Even within my own profession, some psychologists may know that many of their clients report tummy upsets when they are emotionally distressed or anxious, but few would be familiar with the brain-gut axis. In the tenth and most recent edition of *Biological Psychology* – a common textbook for psychology students – there is no mention either of the enteric nervous system, or the brain-gut axis. And yet, we now know that up to ninety-five percent of the body's serotonin (a neurotransmitter that affects mood and digestive function) is found in the gut and in concentrations higher than that found in the brain.

Many researchers into Irritable Bowel Syndrome (IBS) have identified that a large number of IBS sufferers also suffer from psychological distress, including histories of abuse, depression and anxiety.[6] Such findings have led researchers to refer to the gut, or the ENS as the 'little brain'. Gives credibility to the notion of 'gut feelings', doesn't 'it?

Why is this important? Because the research reaffirms the view that the mind-body inter-relationship cannot be separated when trying to understand the factors that contribute to either illness or wellness. Secondly, the role of nutrition in determining our physical and mental health becomes critical. And yet, Western medicine has primarily not concerned itself with this important mind-body interaction, or with nutritional or environmental influences on health. Many doctors in Australia and in overseas developed countries have little training in and little knowledge of either. By contrast, many European and Asian countries have medical traditions that acknowledge both.

It is my firm view that training in nutrition must become an increasing part of the medical and psychological degree courses. Currently such training is either completely missing or woefully inadequate.

In a survey of 100 medical schools in the United States in 2010, in seventy-five percent of the schools students were receiving less than the recommended twenty-five hours training in nutrition over four years and it is known from the profession that few have revisited the subject since graduating. Recently, John McDougall MD authored a Senate bill which would require all doctors in California to include a course in nutrition as part of their continuing professional education, but the Californian Medical Association strongly opposed the bill! It was however subsequently passed in a modified version. Dr McDougall, who has practised medicine for over forty years and whose son graduated from medical school two years ago, held grave concerns about the lack of training in nutrition for medical students that continued to be perpetuated over that forty year period.

Incidentally, the largest source of funding for American medical schools comes from pharmaceutical companies with the curricula set by the AMA.

Most of the major causes of death and illness in the western world today are diet-related, yet most doctors continue to rate their own nutrition knowledge and skills as inadequate. Just recently, I asked some medical students who were doing placements at the aboriginal health service in which I work, how much training in nutrition was part of their medical degree. Their answer was ZERO - no training in nutrition whatsoever, although one student said he had attended one lecture (2 hours) as an undergraduate on vitamin Bs and iron. I find that astounding and alarming, since we are continually told through advertising to consult our doctors in relation to nutritional matters. One writer recently cynically commented that the doctor's receptionist is likely to know more about nutrition from the diets she has been on than the doctor! Of course, many doctors do take an interest in nutrition and attempt to self-educate, but the information available can often be outdated or tainted, particularly if relying on government or industry sources.

'Good nutrition will prevent ninety-five percent of all disease.' Said Linus Pauling, chemist and two-time Nobel Laureate.

His words echo those of Hippocrates, widely accepted as the Father of Medicine, who said sometime around 400BC 'Let food be thy medicine, and medicine be thy food.' Well that would have a dramatic impact on the profitability of drug companies, wouldn't it?

How Healthy is Our Health System?

The increasing levels of chronic illness in the Western world is placing considerable pressure on our health systems and the well-intentioned practitioners working within them. Combined with trends to prescribe medications as the preferred course of treatment, the possibility for human error in health care is greatly increased.

The current levels of iatrogenic deaths in western countries is absolutely mind-boggling and has been called pandemic by a number of authors on the subject. Iatrogenic deaths– (iatros, Greek for physician) – are deaths induced inadvertently by a physician or surgeon, or by medical treatment or diagnostic procedures. John Archer, an Australian investigative journalist and author of a book in 1995 called *Bad Medicine: Is the Health-care System Letting You Down?*, used public domain medical literature to guesstimate that Australia had 50,000 iatrogenic deaths and 750,000 permanent injuries per year.[7]

Ron Law, Executive Director of the NNFA in New Zealand, reported to the British Medical Journal in 2013 that official Australian government reports show that preventable medical error in hospitals is the cause of eleven per cent of all deaths in Australia, which is about one in every nine deaths. If deaths from private practice and properly researched, properly registered, properly prescribed and properly used drugs are included, that figure rises to a staggering nineteen per cent - that's almost one out of every five deaths! [8]

In the United States the figures are even higher, with a report by Dr Barbara Starfield of the John Hopkins School of Hygiene and Public Health reporting the following figures:-

> **ALL THESE ARE DEATHS PER YEAR:**
> - 12,000 -- unnecessary surgery
> - 7,000 -- medication errors in hospitals
> - 20,000 -- other errors in hospitals
> - 80,000 -- infections in hospitals
> - 106,000 -- non-error, negative effects of drugs

A report by the American Institute of Medicine indicated that an estimated 30 percent of all medical procedures, medications and tests, at a cost of $750 billion per year – may in fact be unnecessary.

> "You medical people will have more lives to answer for in the other world than even we generals."
>
> *Napoleon Bonaparte*

By comparison, iatrogenic deaths within the complementary and alternative medicine (CAM) fields have been so few that I have found it difficult to locate figures, though I do recall a media frenzy over ONE death several years ago from an overdose of Kava in a woman who had pre-existing serious illness. This one death prompted a major recall of the supplement and the forced closure of the manufacturer.

CAM continues to come under scrutiny and criticism for not being evidence based, even though the claims made about the evidence of contemporary orthodox medicine *excludes* data of iatrogenesis! You will see from the chart over the page, that you are ten times more likely to die from being struck by lightning, than from taking supplements. In the United States, where more than 60 billion doses of supplements are taken annually, there are *no* recorded deaths.

Maintain a Healthy Mind and Body

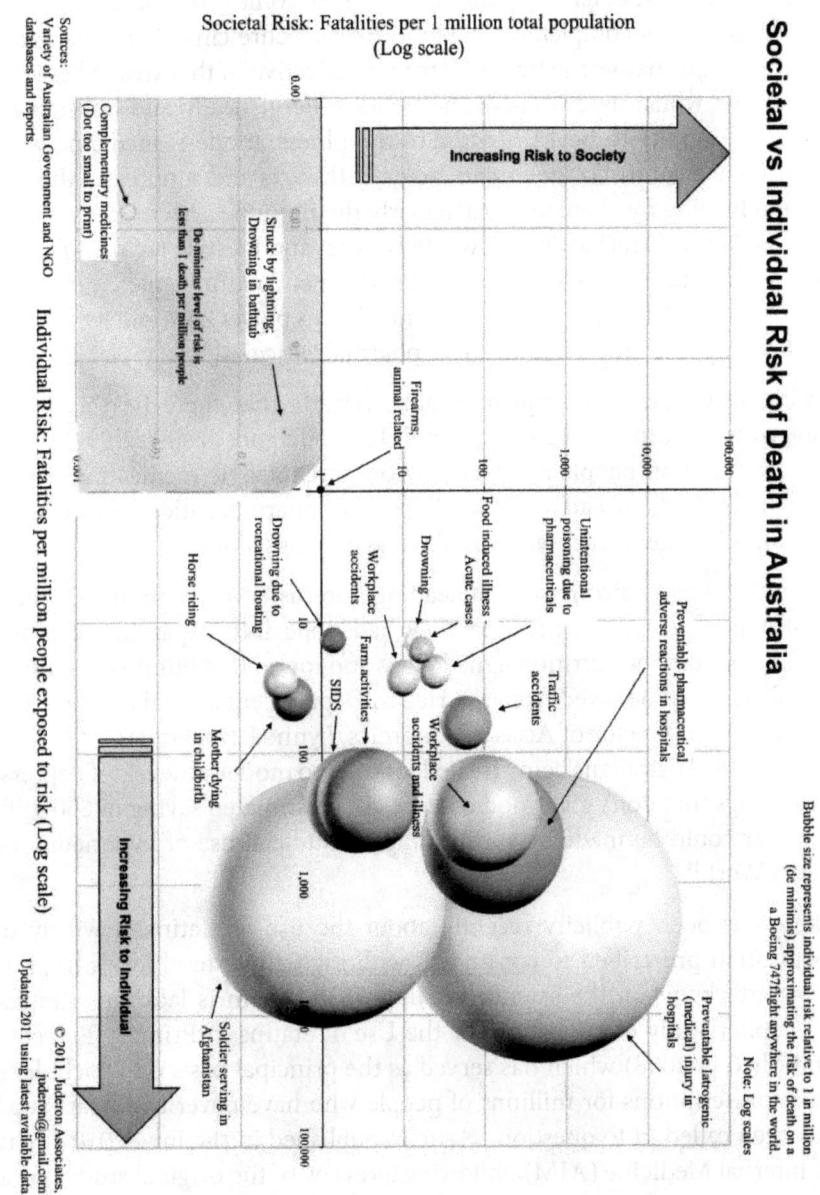

Australian trauma and general surgeon Dr Valerie Malka, former director of trauma services at Sydney's Westmead Hospital, when asked whether universities should teach alternative medicine, was reported as saying that whilst modern medicine is superior when it comes to emergency, trauma and surgery, it is completely unable to treat or cure chronic illness and that natural or alternative medicine is far more effective in this area. She went on to say that whilst natural medicines work synergistically and holistically on the body's ability to heal the *cause* of the illness, modern medicine with its focus on the control of *symptoms*, actually thwarts and suppresses the body's natural healing mechanisms, particularly the immune system, with its liberal use of drugs and its lack of knowledge of diet and lifestyle factors. Dr Malka believes that the moves to discredit alternative and natural medicine may have more to do with the threat to modern medicine's power base and its 'unhealthy relationship' with the 'trillion-dollar pharmaceutical industry'[9].

Phillip Day, researcher and journalist, reports that there has been a four thousand per cent increase in mental illness diagnoses since 1994; that one hundred million people are currently on psychotropic medications; 42,000 are killed by them each year, and that the pharmaceutical companies are making $7.7 billion each *day* on this class of drugs alone.[10]

Recently, Access Economics, a leading forecaster of economic trends in Australia, reported on research they had done into expanding the use of complementary or nutritional medicines and found that hundreds of millions of dollars could be saved from the Health Department annual budget. As one example, the Director of Access Economics, Lynne Pezzullo, reported that for the 340,000 Australians being treated for mild to moderate levels of depression with drugs that don't give good outcomes, an estimated saving of $50 million per year could be made by substituting the judicial use of hypericum, or St John's Wort.[11]

There has been publicity recently about the use of statins, a widely used medication prescribed to consumers with high cholesterol levels to prevent heart attacks when the science to support the claim is lacking. Results of the Jupiter study (Justification for the Use of Statins in Primary Prevention, published in 2008) which has served as the principal basis on which doctors write prescriptions for millions of people who have never had heart attacks, has been called in to question. Articles published in the June 2010 Archives of Internal Medicine (AIM), following a review of the original study revealed 'Potential ethical, clinical and financial conflicts of interest at work in the execution of the Jupiter study' with the scientists concluding that the original trial was 'flawed' and raised 'troubling questions concerning the role of commercial sponsors.' In addition, the benchmark for cholesterol levels, which established the cut off point for those deemed to be at-risk was lowered overnight in the United States, which meant that millions of people, who the day before had cholesterol levels within the safe range were suddenly moved into the at risk range though there was no actual change in their cholesterol levels.

The deliberate lowering of the benchmarks meant that an additional twenty-three million people became candidates for statin use, offering huge financial rewards to the manufacturers. Eight of the nine panel members who established the new guidelines had industry ties, prompting an independent group of more than thirty scientists to write to the National Institutes of Health vigorously publicly opposing the recommendations.[12] Such conflicts of interest are sadly becoming commonplace.

In spite of the apparent lagging behind of sections of the medical profession, health consumers in Western countries have led the way in demanding a more integrated or holistic approach to their health care and this has begun to be embraced within some sections of the medical profession.

Dr Malka says 'It is about time the Australian medical profession started educating rather than medicating. It is unfortunate that it is the public's disillusionment with modern medicine and its inability to treat many diseases, as well as the dreadful side-effects of any treatment offered, that have increased the popularity of complementary and alternative medicine. It should have been due to the interest, enthusiasm and reason of doctors, scientists, researchers and politicians. As a qualified medical specialist and surgeon, I am ashamed of the medical profession when it so blatantly displays its ignorance and persists in attacking a profession from which we have much to learn.'[13]

It is my hope that the natural medicine industry and its practitioners continue to work collaboratively with contemporary, orthodox medicine practitioners in the mutual interests of achieving the best possible outcomes for patients and for the health of our society generally. However, it can often be difficult for health professionals such as me, let alone the general population to make sense of the vast amount of information in relation to what is good nutritionally.

There is a plethora of information in newspapers, magazines, and online about which foods to eat and which to avoid, and much of the information seems contradictory and confusing. In recent weeks, for example, I have seen headlines telling us dairy is bad, dairy is good, margarine is bad, butter is good, fats are good, fats are bad, soy is good, soy is bad, whole wheat is good, whole wheat is toxic, etc., etc., etc. One of the reasons that this happens is because the scientific field of nutrition is a relatively new science and there is still a great deal that we do not understand about how nutrients work, particularly synergistically within individual digestive systems. Micahel Pollan in his book *In Defense of Food,* traces the history of what he calls 'nutritionism', the reduction of food to the sum of its nutrients, and notes this quasi-scientific approach to food is causing considerable anxiety for those eating the western diet. He refers to this food anxiety as *orthorexia* – from the Greek 'ortho' (right and correct) + 'exia' (appetite) = right appetite. Pollan argues that the United States is becoming a nation of *orthorexics*: people with an unhealthy obsession with eating healthily and proposes that it should be added to the DSM (The Diagnostic and Statistical Manual of Mental Disorders).[14]

Certainly within my own clinics I see many people who are anxious about what to eat and this is a relatively new phenomena. Consumers are confused by the mixed messages that seem to be coming from those involved in nutrition including health professionals, the food industry and government and it is not surprising. Much of the research is either tainted by conflicts of interest, or is simply too reductionist – reducing food to individually isolated nutrients. With such alarming trends in the declining health of our young people and the dramatic escalation of chronic illness including mental illness, we need an independent food safety authority, but until then, what can we do?

What Can We Do to Ensure Good Nutrition for Ourselves, Our Families and Future Generations?

Firstly, *don't feel overwhelmed*. Food production has increasingly been taken out of our hands and we have lost control over how our food is grown and processed with much of it now being chemically altered, devoid of vital nutrients and in some cases toxic. But there are things we can do to improve our knowledge and understanding of basic nutritional principles. With a greater level of awareness, we are less likely to be hoodwinked by food producers who may have different agendas.

Essentially, our bodies require three types of nutrients - fats, carbohydrates and proteins and it is helpful if we know and understand the difference between fats that are metabolically important and those that are harmful; and about the glycaemic index (GI) of carbohydrates. Everybody's DNA is different and will process nutrients in different ways and nutrients work synergistically together in ways that we do not yet understand. So, as with the rest of this book, I do not wish to be too prescriptive in what you should or shouldn't eat, but will include instead some general guidelines for achieving and maintaining optimal health based on the latest nutritional and environmental medicine research.

The Principles

1. **Eat food that is as natural as possible**, in its original form, grown in a natural environment, free of pesticides and herbicides and any genetic modification or changes. Choose foods from the three major groups of nutrients – fats, carbohydrates and proteins. Eating foods as close to its natural state, in the season it is normally grown and preferably grown locally, is called 'clean' food, or 'clean' eating. If you can grow your own, this is best. You know exactly what you are getting and can enrich your soils by composting. You can grow foods seasonally in accordance with their natural preference for heat, cold, wet, dry conditions.

If you are a meat-eater try to source organic or chemical-free meats and poultry that are grass rather than grain fed.

Many animals are raised these days on grains including corn and the inclusion of corn oil into much of our food supply has contributed to the raising of omega-6 fatty acids. Pasture-raised animals that subsist largely on grasses have lower levels of omega-6, but also higher levels of omega-3.

Grass fed beef cattle also have lower levels of saturated fatty acids, which can contribute to lower cholesterol levels in people who consume the meat from these animals, compared with grain-fed animals.

2. **Eat more fresh, organic fruits and vegetables.** Once again, if you can grow your own fruits and vegetables, particularly if you are feeding young children, that is a great way to increase the range of nutrients and decrease your levels of ingestion of toxic chemicals. You can juice fruits and vegetables to increase your intake, but be careful not to juice too much fruit, because of the high fructose levels, which will act on the body in a similar way to sucrose. Eat as many different coloured vegetables as you can each day in order to take full advantage of the range of vitamins and minerals. Try to eat the majority of your vegetables raw rather than cooked since many vitamins and minerals are destroyed during heating. Make your plates a veritable kaleidoscope of colour. Your children will enjoy this and learn so much about different foods.

3. **Stop dieting, weighing your food and counting calories.** There is plenty of evidence to show that dieting does not work. Instead, relax and enjoy a broad range of fresh foods in moderation.

4. **Increase your supply of Omega-3** rich foods including oily fish, walnuts, linseed or flaxseed either ground or as oil. But be careful not to expose the

oils to sunlight, as they will deteriorate and go rancid quickly. Simply by eating more green leafy vegetables and less refined oils and processed foods you will be restoring the ratio of Omega-3 to Omega-6 Essential Fatty Acids (EFAs) to much healthier levels.

World's Healthiest Foods rich in omega-3 fats

Food	Cals%	Daily Value
Flax Seeds, ground	75	132.9%
Walnuts	164	94.5%
Salmon	245	61.2%
Sardines	189	55.8%
Beef, grass-fed	175	45.8%
Soybeans	298	42.9%
Halibut	159	25.8%
Scallops	127	17%
Shrimp	112	15.4%
Tofu	86	15%

Table from the world's healthiest foods website: www. whfoods.org

5. **Avoid highly processed foods** – they are nearly always filled with sugar, salt and chemicals and have little nutritional content.

6. **Reduce your exposure to toxins** – choose to grow your own fruits and vegetables, or choose organically grown. Reduce your exposure to chemicals in household products – cleaning products and personal care products. Give up smoking and reduce consumption of alcohol and sugar. Seek assistance if you have any addictions.

7. **Learn to cook** – it is generally healthier and considerably cheaper to cook at home than it is to buy take-away food, or to eat in restaurants. Clean eating recipes are often simple and easy, but also nutritious and delicious. Learning about which foods work together, about herbs and spices, about food from different cultures and getting creative in the kitchen, can be good fun and very rewarding. Most children love to be involved in food preparation and cooking and you will be setting them up for a positive and healthy relationship with

food in the future. In addition to teaching them to love and respect food, they get to spend time with you and learn some cooking skills that will stand them in good stead for when the time comes for them to live independently.

Most public libraries have an excellent range of cook books and I have also found the internet very helpful. You can key in a specific ingredient into a search engine, or search for a particular dish and get some great ideas. You can specify in your search if you require the recipe to be gluten-free, dairy-free, or for it to accommodate other allergies or sensitivities.

8. **Take time to eat mindfully** – don't rush or eat on the go. Do whatever you can to take time out to eat rather than eating at your desk, in your car, down the street, etc. Savour the food that you are eating and be thankful for the nutrients that are fuelling and repairing your body.

9. **Enjoy eating with others** – make eating a social event as it was for many in the past. Think of ways that you can have rituals around food, for example, special ways of setting the table – a crisp, clean table cloth, candles, flowers, elegant cutlery and crockery etc. Sadly, for many families the tradition of all sitting together at the family dining table has been lost. Sharing a meal and conversation is not just good for digestion, but for mental health, and for the soul.

10. **Eat only when hungry and stop when full.**

11. **Take a good vitamin and mineral supplement** if you are unable to grow your own food, or access local, organically grown produce.

Be careful to buy only a reputable brand and if you can, get your natural therapist's view on the product, since the quality of some over-the-counter 'natural' medicines can be variable, with doses below therapeutic or recommended levels and some can also contain fillers. In particular, consider the need to increase your Vitamin D intake, as many of us are deficient and it is essential for maintaining a healthy immune system. The darker your skin, the greater your requirement for Vitamin D. Consult a health practitioner with up to date training in metabolic, orthomolecular, or nutritional medicine for more specific advice.

12. **Don't feel bad about anything you eat.** All foods are nutrients, especially to a starving person, and you want to aim to develop a positive relationship with food, rather than having food associated with negative feelings like shame, guilt and fear. Most of us have some idea about the types of food we should eat for good health, and the foods we should avoid or minimise to prevent ill-health. Try to become as conscious as possible about your

choices. Occasionally we will make a decision to eat a food that we know is not particularly nutrient-rich or good for us, but we should not beat ourselves up for this. As long as we are eating healthy, nutritious foods most of the time, and enjoy our occasional departures, that's fine. Remember vibrational alignment: be in vibrational alignment with what you DO want (healthy, disease-free body and mind) rather than with what you DON'T want (illness, obesity). So remember to enjoy all that your food has to offer.

Just as I believe that we have contributed to an explosion in the prevalence of mental health disorders by talking and focussing so much on them, I think we have also talked up obesity and obsession with food to a point where so many people, including our children, are apprehensive and even afraid around food.

If we are a not in vibrational alignment when eating food, if we believe the food we eat is bad for us, it will be expressed this way in our bodies. If you are going to have that chocolate, or piece of cake occasionally, then enjoy it as food for your soul.

Quite simply, we need to enjoy the abundance of clean food we have in our country compared with many other places, and give thanks for it. We can grow more of it ourselves, reduce the high levels of chemicalisation, and increase the levels of minerals, vitamins and trace elements, thereby providing good nutrition for ourselves and for future generations.

13. Drink plenty of clean water

14. Get involved in demanding change in the approach to food production and manufacturing. Lobby government for restrictions and changes that are pro-health, and boycott unethical or high polluting companies.

The evidence of the link between changes to our food supply and to elevating levels of so many chronic diseases is overwhelming, yet our governments have been slow to respond. As parents, as health consumers, we must start demanding that our food is made clean and toxin free – we must demand that our governments stand apart from the financial interests of big business and protect our health and safety, and hold corporations involved in food production and medicine accountable. Government legislative, investigative, reporting and regulatory processes and structures must be as free of potential conflicts of interest as possible and we must start boycotting companies that act dishonestly, or in their own self-interest cause harm to the consumer.

I hope the information in this chapter serves to encourage you to become more actively involved in your own health and nutrition. It has not been my intention to frighten you, but rather to inform you so that you are able to make your own decisions in the best interests of optimal health.

We need to hold our governments, food producers and medical practitioners to account and ensure that the values of honesty, integrity, and care and concern for all are integral. The evidence is overwhelming – good nutrition and exercise will strengthen your immune system and reduce inflammation and chronic illness and that is what we *do* want, and want to focus our attention on.

If you are currently experiencing low mood, however, here are some foods that may contribute to raising your serotonin levels and other mood enhancing neurotransmitters for some relief:

Top Mood Boosting Foods
- Bananas (Trypophan, B6, Potassium)
- Green, leafy vegetables (Folate and B Vitamins)
- Oily Fish – Mackerel, Sardines, Salmon, Barramundi (Omega 3)
- Walnuts and Turkey (Tryptophan)
- Dark Chocolate (Phenylethylamine (PEA)*, Antioxidants)
- Avoid sugar, caffeine and alcohol

This is the chemical your brain creates when you feel you are falling in love. PEA encourages your brain to release endorphins (feel-good chemicals.)

The Importance of Exercise
Our bodies and brains are designed for forward movement and we need some form of regular physical exercise in order to maintain good physical and emotional health.

As little as thirty minutes exercise three times a week – brisk walking, for example – is sufficient to keep our levels of serotonin high enough to prevent mood disorders and gastric disturbance.

Several studies have also shown that people who exercise regularly experience less brain volume loss and neuronal decline as they age, with one study showing that people older than sixty who participated in six months of aerobic exercise, developed significantly greater thickness of the cortex, especially in the frontal lobes, compared with those who did not participate. (Cortical thinning is associated with ageing and with dementia).

A recent, ground-breaking study published in the British Medical journal found that exercise achieved similar results to medications in preventing and treating heart failure and heart disease, and also in diabetes prevention.

Exercise proved more helpful than drug treatment to people who had suffered stroke, and it caused fewer side effects and injuries. Yet the researchers noted also that medication prescription rates had increased sharply in England between 2000 and 2010, while only fourteen percent of adults reported exercising regularly.[15]

In an American study in 2008,[16] it was shown that people aged between sixty and eighty years, who aerobically exercised at least three hours a week over the course of ten years showed:

- An increase in the number of large blood vessels in the cerebral region of the brain
- An increase in blood flow in the three major cerebral arteries

The cerebral area controls consciousness, memory, initiation of activity, emotional response, language and word associations. Narrowing and loss of blood vessels may be associated with cognitive decline.

And finally, in a study evaluating the relative effectiveness of three different treatments for Major Depressive Disorder comprising i)anti-depressant medication (Zoloft), ii)anti-depressant medication combined with physical exercise and iii)physical exercise only, showed after four months that 60 to 70 percent of the participants were 'vastly improved' or 'symptom free' across all three conditions.

On a ten month follow up, however,

- 38% of Zoloft condition subjects had recurrence of depression
- 31% of the combined Zoloft plus exercise condition had recurrence of depression
- 8% of the exercise-only condition had recurrence (and people who continued to exercise were less likely as a group to have recurrence).[17]

As people become more informed about the factors that influence their health, I am hopeful that there will continue to be a consumer-lead demand for increasing honesty in medicine and collaboration between orthodox Western medicine and complementary and alternative medicine (CAM), as well as an increase in quality, independent research into alternatives to drug therapy. Increased collaboration between the two approaches will, I suspect, allow a more comprehensive and holistic approach to combatting the factors that contribute to illness in the twenty-first century. It will also address better the factors that enhance wellbeing, including environmental and nutritional influences and the patient's role in their own health care.

So, now it is time for you to rate your current state of physical and emotional health and to consider goals for maximising positive health and wellbeing.

My Health and Wellbeing Inventory
On a scale of 0 – 5, where 0 = very poor and 5 = excellent:

How would I rate my current overall health?   0   1   2   3   4   5

What would need to be different for me to have optimal general health?

My goal for the next month is:

_____

How would you rate your current mental health?   0   1   2   3   4   5

What would need to be different for me to have optimal mental health?

My goal for the next month is:

_____

How would you rate your current nutrition?   0   1   2   3   4   5

What changes would I need to make to be eating more nutritious foods?

My goal for the next month is:

_____

How would you rate your current level of exercise: 0   1   2   3   4   5

What changes would I need to make to improve my level of fitness?

My goal for the next month is:

_____

(Endnotes)

1. Schroeder, Henry R. "Losses of Vitamins and Trace Minerals Resulting from Processing and Preservation of Foods," *American Journal of Clinical Nutrition*, 1971
2. Sacks, Gary. *Big Food Lobbying: tip of the iceberg exposed.* http://theconversation.com 19th February, 2014.
3. Hardell L, Carlberg M, Mild KH. Use of mobile phones and cordless phones is associated with increased risk for lioma and acoustic neuroma. *Pathophysiology.* (2012), in press.
4. Hibbeln, J. cited in Lawrence, F. "Omega-3, junk food and the link between violence and what we eat". *The Guardian,* October 17, 2006.
5. **Jacka, Felice N.**, Ystrom, Eivind*, Brantsaeter, Anne Lise*, Karevold, Evalill*, Roth, Christine*, Haugen, Margaretha*, Meltzer, Helle Margrete*, Schjolberg, Synnve* and Berk, Michael (2013) Maternal and early postnatal nutrition and mental health of offspring by age 5 years: a prospective cohort study clinical guidance, *Journal of the American academy of child & pdolescent psychiatry*, vol. 52, no. 10, pp. 1038-1047, Elsevier, Amsterdam, The Netherlands [C1.1] ERA journal ID: 6483 – Scopus EID: 2-s2.0-84884903219
6. Mach, T. The brain-gut axis in irritable bowel syndrome – clinical aspects. *Med Sci Monit.* 2004 1-0(6):125-131 and Baker, DE., Rationale for using serotonergic agents to treat irritable bowel syndrome .*Am J Health-Syst Pharm.* 2005 62:700-711
7. Archer, J. *Bad Medicine: Is the Health-Care System Letting You Down?* Simon & Schuster: Aust. 1995.
8. Iatrogenic Injury in Australia – A Report prepared by the Australian Patient Safety Foundation for the Department of Health and Aged Care. Commonwealth Government of Australia, August, 2001.
9. Malka, Valerie. Opinion interview - Should Universities Teach Alternative Medicine? 14th Accessed October, 2013.http://www.smh.com.au/opinion
10. Day, Phillip. From Australian Tour: What's News? Examining the Latest in Nutritional and Metabolic Breakthroughs, Melbourne, 27th October, 2013.
11. Brighthope, I. "The Forces Against Health in Australia". Accessed August, 2013. http://www.orthomolecular.org
12. http://www.alternet.org/personal-health/misconceptions-about-statins. Accessed 2nd October, 2013.
13. Malka, Valerie. Opinion interview - Should Universities Teach Alternative Medicine? 14th Accessed October, 2013.http://www.smh.com.au/opinion
14. Pollan, Michael. *In Defense of Food: An Eater's Manifesto.* (USA: Gale, Cengage Learning, 2009.
15. Naci H, Ioannidis JPA. Comparative effectiveness of exercise and drug interventions on mortality outcomes: metaepidemiological study. *British Medical Study.* Published online October 1, 2013.
16. Rahman, Feraz, et. al (2008). Study presented at Radiological Society of North America; UNC Chapel Hill researchers.
17. Blumenthal, James A. Phd et al. "Exercise and Pharmacology in the Treatment of Major Depressive Disorder". *Psychomatic Medicine* 69:587-596 (2007).

Chapter 12 – Invest in Positive Relationships

As the research into sustainable happiness indicates, positive relationships play a significant role in our sense of wellbeing. A new and innovative study at the Sahlgrenska Academy and Lund University in Sweden found that the words most associated with the word 'happiness' were words that related to people and relationships, rather than to material things. In Indigenous Australia, family relationships are fundamental to wellbeing and incorporate a complex system of obligation and reciprocity that ties kin together in ways we have difficulty comprehending.

Yet, in spite of the importance to us of social relationships, statistics from the United States indicate that over the past twenty five years:-

- Shared family dinners have declined 43%
- Having friends over to the house has declined 35%
- Participation in clubs and civic organisations has decreased by 58%
- The average American has only two close friends and one in four (25%) report they have no-one to confide in.[1]

We are social beings. Our brains are wired to be in social relationships, so what is the status of our relationships currently and what can we do to improve them?

The factors that enhance our relationships, whether personal, intimate, or work-based, are:

- Self awareness
- Empathy
- Positive Communication
- Mutual Respect

The more we know about ourselves, the more likely we are to understand our responses to others.

Whatever is going on inside our heads and bodies comes into play in our closest relationships. The more we can know and understand what these forces are, the more we can accept responsibility for them; we can reduce their influence if they are negative aspects; we can increase their presence if they are positive aspects. Remember, no-one is responsible for our feelings but us – ever.

Spheres or Bubbles of Perception
When we come into contact with another person, our world comes into play with their world. (See Bubbles or Spheres of Perception diagram.) Inside each of us is our own unique set of Beliefs, Values, Fears, Needs, Thoughts, Feelings, and Life Experiences. When we enter a relationship with another, our world comes into contact with their world of *their* own unique set of Beliefs, Values, Fears, Needs, Thoughts, Feelings and Life Experiences.

In friendships and intimate relationships we are often drawn to someone because some of their "world" or "Bubble" matches what is in our own. For example, I may be drawn towards someone who shares my commitment to the values of equality and integrity, or I may be attracted to someone who has grown up in a large family, as I have. However, no matter how many similarities we find between us, there will always be differences too, and it is these differences that either enrich or destroy relationships. The *acceptance* of difference is critical for successful relationships.

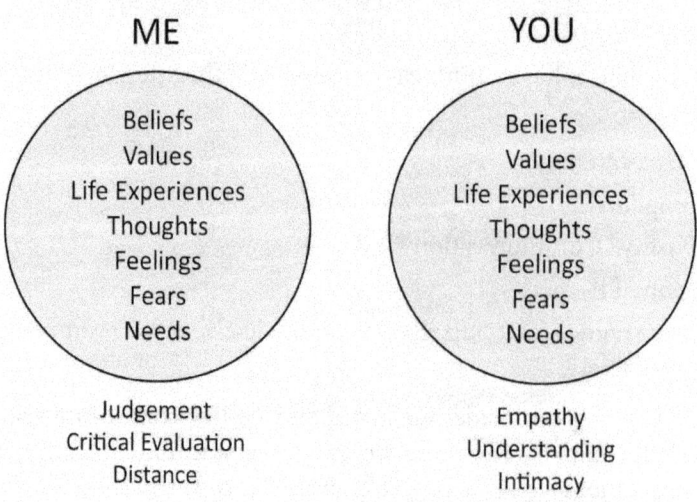

It is our job to get to know as much as we can about our own bubble of perception. You have already done some exercises earlier, that have helped to clarify your values and beliefs, your thoughts and feelings, and examine your needs or future expectations. But how do we find out about what is going on for others with whom we are in relationship? The answer is through building empathy, and we cannot develop empathy if we stand firmly within our own bubbles, whilst we relate to others. If we do so, we will mentally filter *their* stories through *our* own sets of beliefs, values, life experiences, etc., which may be very different to theirs. This can only lead to us making judgements and critically evaluating (against *our* criteria). If this happens frequently, it will lead to distance.

In clinic I often hear partners say, 'He never listens to me'; or 'She just doesn't understand me.' In order to develop empathy, we need to leave our bubbles and jump into the other person's bubble, in other words, *suspend judgement* and adopt a position of *genuine curiosity* about why the person you are engaged with holds the views they do. This can often be facilitated by asking open questions. (Open questions are questions that elicit more than a simple Yes/No answer. For example, rather than, 'Are you feeling angry?' you might ask, 'Can you tell me what it is you are feeling?').

When we suspend judgement and stand within our partner's or other person's bubble, and respectfully listen and accept what they say, we provide the conditions that will lead to increased empathy and understanding and, over time, increased intimacy. By intimacy I mean trust and connection: being able to share more and more personal information that we would not share with others with whom we felt less of a connection, or less safety. Attitudes of openness, honesty, responsibility and a willingness to commit to positive communication is essential.

The Importance of Communication for All Relationships

In the thirteenth century, Emperor Frederick of Germany wanted to know what language had been spoken at the birth of mankind in the Garden of Eden. He ordered an experiment where fifty newborn babies were raised without human interaction so as to determine what language they might naturally speak if isolated from hearing human speech. Salimbene, an Italian Franciscan friar and chronicler, wrote in his Chronicles that King Frederick instructed 'foster-mothers and nurses to suckle and bathe and wash the children, but in no ways to prattle or speak with them; for he would have learnt whether they would speak the Hebrew language (which had been the first), or Greek, or Latin, or Arabic, or perchance the tongue of their parents of whom they had been born.....'

What do you imagine the results would have been?

The infants didn't speak at all? – This is what most people answer when I ask them this question when I am facilitating workshops in communications skills.

No.

The infants spoke gibberish – grunts and noises, but no discernible words?

No.

In fact, the results of the experiment were - that all fifty babies died.

Communication is so vital to our healthy development and wellbeing, that the lack of it is toxic and can be lethal. Have any of you had the experience of being given 'the silent treatment', where someone (usually someone you care about) withdraws all forms of communication, because they are angry with you? If you have, you will know just how painful this form of punishment can be. Research confirms that children would rather be yelled at than ignored by their parents, and that victims of abuse would rather be physically abused than ignored. There is a reason why solitary confinement is considered to be a particularly brutal form of punishment within the prison system. The silent treatment, is a passive-aggressive form of abuse. It conveys disapproval and contempt through silent gestures and periods of verbal silence. This is different to the notion of being quiet, or taking time out, which can be a very effective way of dealing with overwhelming emotion. A good summary of the differences outlined in the chart that follows, has been put together by a website to support people living with someone with a personality disorder, www.outofthefog.net

	Time-Out	**Silent Treatment**
Effect	Constructive	Destructive
Duration	Time Bound	Indefinite
Non-Verbals	Neutral or Reassuring	Contemptuous
Physical Posture	Disengaged	Engaged
Re-engagement	Mutually Agreed	Unilateral
Engagement of Third Parties	To seek self-support	To seek alliances in the argument.
Disposition	Seeks self-improvement	Seeks to improve others
Problem Focus	To find solutions	To apportion blame

Invest in Positive Relationships

Although many people I see in clinic believe that the silent treatment is the same as not communicating, they are wrong. It is powerfully communicating contempt – that you are not even worth being acknowledged, you are not worthy of my breath or attention. This form of communication is also toxic and will lead to the death of your relationship. If you are using the silent treatment in your relationships, you must take responsibility to stop.

So, positive communication skills are essential for successful relationships, and interpersonal communication (verbal and non-verbal) is one of humanity's greatest accomplishments, yet many of us have learnt unhelpful ways of communicating about our feelings and our needs. Fortunately, research studies indicate that people of all ages are capable of learning specific communication skills which will lead to enhanced personal relationships and increased competence in the workplace, and my clinical work confirms this.

Essentially, there are three stages in the process of communicating to another:

1. **Transmitting or sending a message**
2. **Receiving (hearing) a message**
3. **Interpreting or Decoding a message**

The Communication Process

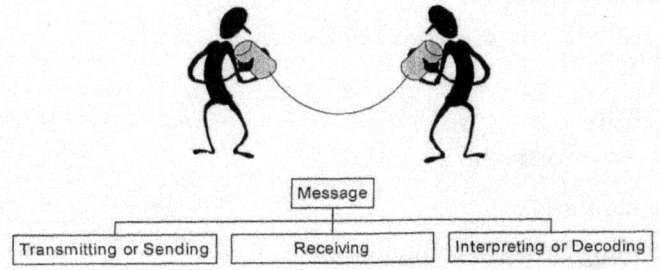

Stage 1 – Sending the message requires both verbal and non-verbal cues and for communication to be clear, the non-verbal must be congruent, i.e. match up with the verbal. You can not say to your partner, 'I'm fine' in a terse tone while slamming things around and expect them to believe that you are, in fact, fine. For most of us, sending a message is relatively uncomplicated.

Stage 2 – Receiving the message: again, for most of us, receiving or hearing a message is not difficult. But sometimes we are distracted and do not pay full attention. At other times, particularly if the subject of conversation is a difficult one, or brings up strong emotion for us, we are mentally rehearsing what we are going to say next, rather than paying full attention to what our partner is saying.

Listening For Understanding
Attending Skills
Show that you are available, ready and interested to hear your partner

- Define your availability
- Create suitable space
- Attend to immediate needs (so that these do not become distractions)
- Eye contact
- Attentive posture
- Verbal and non-verbal encouragements

Following Skills
Encourages your partner to go on

- Invitations
- Avoiding blocks to communication
- Minimal encouragements
- Open questions
- Empathic silence

Reflective Listening Skills

Listen attentively without responding or judging. At the speaker's conclusion, restate in your own words, both the feeling and the content of that person's communication, so as to demonstrate understanding and acceptance.

- Paraphrasing
- Reflecting content and feelings
- Summarising

Some useful phrases in paraphrasing or reflecting can include....

- It seems that....
- You feel......
- From where you stand.......
- You mean........
- In other words......

Stage 3 – Interpreting or Decoding the message – this is where 'miscommunication' or misunderstanding can occur. The message we have sent has been received and then filtered by the listener through their own bubble of perception, and they may have arrived at conclusions other than what we intended.

An example of this miscommunication that I often use during my training sessions comes from a group session that I was running some years ago for a group of long-term unemployed people of mixed gender and ages ranging from seventeen to fifty-seven years. I was talking to the group about anti-discrimination legislation and what sorts of questions were not appropriate for employers to ask and I gave a brief introduction to what sexual harassment in the workplace was. At this point, the oldest person in the group, a fifty-seven year old unemployed man, who had been retrenched after working all his life in the petro-chemical industry, said, 'Oh, I would love to be sexually harassed!' There were a couple of giggles, but then the youngest member of the group, a seventeen year old young woman, leapt to her feet, and with a flushed face yelled, 'Well you're a f......g creep!' and marched out of the room. At this, the fifty-seven year old male became very confused and appeared genuinely concerned that he had upset the young woman. We took a break and later the young woman came to see me. She apologised for her outburst, and explained her reaction to what had been said.

Now, if we return to the communication process – the fifty-seven year old man **sent** his message effectively, everyone in the room **received** or heard the message. But there was a variety of **interpretations** or reactions. Why? How did this happen? It happened because of the filtering of the message that took place within each person's bubble of perception. The fifty-seven year old man, who had worked all his life in a male-dominated workplace, heard 'sexual harassment' and interpreted from his world, his bubble of perception, 'sexual desirability'.

The young woman explained to me that she had just left home that week after suffering years of sexual abuse from her step-father. When she heard the words 'sexual harassment', she interpreted the words from her world, her bubble of perception, as meaning long-term painful and distressing sexual assault.

One very simple, yet powerfully effective technique for reducing the chances of these miscommunications happening is to use a technique called 'Reflective Listening'. Using this simple technique I have seen couples on the verge of divorce completely turn their marriages around and finally hear and understand what their partner is trying to communicate, often for the first time in many years. Incidentally, when I talk about 'partner' I mean child, friend, parent, work colleague, or any other form of relationship; the technique works equally effectively across all domains.

Reflective Listening
Reflective listening involves summarising and feeding back to the Speaker what you as Listener have heard, in order to check that you have properly received the message that was intended. The Speaker's message may include information and emotion and it is important to understand both. Messages may also contain verbal and non-verbal information.

Active or Reflective Listening Exercise

1. Nominate one person to be Speaker, the other to be Listener

2. The Speaker: Keep sentences short, use "I" statements where possible and stick to one issue at a time.

3. The Listener: Listen without interrupting to the Speaker's message and feelings. When the Speaker has finished speaking, summarise what you have heard and reflect this back including any feelings, for example:

'So you are saying that when I come home late you feel angry because dinner gets ruined and you would like me to telephone you to let you know when I can be expected. Is that right?'

4. The Speaker will then indicate to the Listener if they have understood correctly. If they have, you swap roles – the Speaker is the Listener, the Listener will become the Speaker and repeat the above three steps.

If the Listener has not correctly heard what the Speaker intended, the Speaker sends the message again and the Listener reflects back again. This is repeated until the Speaker feels that the Listener has properly understood the message.

Self-awareness, good listening skills and reflective listening are the foundations of effective communication and positive relationships. If practised regularly they will increase understanding and empathy, reduce miscommunications and, ultimately, increase closeness, trust, and intimacy.

It is beyond the scope of this book to address the full range of positive communication skills, but I have referenced a couple of excellent books at the back of this volume should you be interested to follow this topic up further. Many counselling or welfare organisations conduct communication skills workshops. You can also express interest in having a communications skills workshop run in your area by contacting me through my website.

Whilst interacting with others will bring to light both our similarities and our differences, it is often our differences that become the source of conflict, because we want the other person to change to be more like us. Remember from chapter 4 though, we cannot ever change anyone else, we can only change our thinking about them or their behaviour. Differences have to be accepted, or they will destroy the positive aspects of the relationship. However, all relationships must also be based on the principle of mutual respect, hence healthy relationships do not include any form of abuse. In answering the *Inventory of Relationships* questionnaire, consider the following:

1. How healthy are my current relationships?

Do my personal relationships make a positive contribution to my life, or do they diminish the quality of my life? If they diminish my quality of life, can I do anything to change this?

2. Do I have someone that I can talk to about the things that matter most to me?

Can I share the important aspects of my personality, my fears, my needs, my feelings and desires with another and feel understood and supported? Can this person support my vision of what I want for my life?

3. **How many people do I have around me who I can trust to support me in times of need?**

When we work with children, we often ask them to draw around their hand and then think of a person for each finger who they could trust to get help from if they needed it. I think this is an important concept for adults too. This question may have you thinking beyond the most intimate or personal relationships and may include neighbours or work colleagues as support people. These relationships make a valuable contribution to our feelings of safety and wellbeing. If you do not have a positive relationship with your family, or you have lost family members through bereavement, consider "adopting" someone else's family. Most well-functioning families are happy to make room for another member.

4. **Do I feel respected and valued in my relationships?**
   - With my spouse/partner
   - With my children
   - With my broader family
   - With my work colleagues
   - With my friends

If there are any relationships that you feel do not respect and value you, is there something you can do to change this? Ask yourself, 'Can I be myself in this particular relationship, or does the success of the relationship require that I not give expression to all that I feel and all that I can be or do? Am I compromising or accommodating to the needs of others too greatly or too often and feeling resentful?'

5. **Are there any relationships that violate my values or are toxic?**

Relationships that violate our primary values are very challenging. Conflict around values leads more than anything else to the most intense and destructive disagreements.

Sometimes it can be best to simply acknowledge that these relationships are not respectful or supportive and therefore not sustainable.

A Word About Introverts Versus Extroverts

There is much in the general psychology and the happiness literature that affirms the importance of social relationships for positive wellbeing. Much of the literature has, I believe, a bias towards extroversion; even some of the questionnaires designed to measure levels of happiness or life satisfaction seem to have been constructed from an extrovert point of view.

Introverts often have less need for social interaction than do extroverts, or they give expression to this need in a different way. For example, an introvert may have only a few key personal relationships, feel perfectly happy and supported within this context, and have little need for social interaction with work colleagues, community members or extended family members. This is not a short-coming, and yet many introverts are placed under pressure by extroverts to 'come out of their shells' and engage in more social activity than they are naturally inclined toward or comfortable with. We live in an extroverted world, full of activity and noise. It is easy to underestimate or overlook the contribution and preferences of introverts in our world, who, in a recent survey, were shown to number slightly over half the total population. A greater understanding and appreciation of the interior world of the introvert, the differences in needs and the vital contributions that are made through their introspection, quiet reflection and deep contemplation are necessary to modulate this fast-paced, fast-talking, busy world. Then, perhaps, we would stop seeing introversion as pathology and introverts as disordered extroverts requiring therapy.

If your introversion does not stop you from doing what you want to do, there is no cause for concern.

However, if you find yourself avoiding people, places and situations that *you would prefer to experience*, you may need some professional assistance to overcome your shyness, anxiety or social phobia.

Nurturing Your Positive Relationships
Just as we need to service our vehicles regularly in order to get the best performance, we need to service and maintain our key relationships on a regular basis too. Making your most valued relationships your number one priority is essential – nothing must seem to be more important than nurturing the people who contribute to the enrichment of our lives.

- Make regular time for nurturing your primary relationships. Give regular time to doing things that you and your partner/children/friend enjoy. Allow time for conversations, quiet reflection, just being together.
- Take responsibility for your own emotions and needs and regularly communicate them openly and clearly.
- Always focus on and give thanks for the positive aspects of your relationship and the person or people within it.
- Always treat yourself and others with respect.

- Give regular positive feedback to the people you are involved with and tell them what it is about them that you value and appreciate. Some ways of doing this include sending notes, leaving messages on whiteboards, putting sticky-notes with loving messages up in places they are likely to see them; for example, on the bathroom mirror.
- Accept and respect difference. You cannot change others; focus your attention instead on their positive qualities. If you feel your values are compromised, the respectful thing to do may be to end the relationship.
- Practice kindness and compassion.
- Learn how to say 'NO'. Always say 'YES' with a full heart.

  Remember, just as you alone are responsible for your feelings and happiness, so it is for others. You are not responsible for their feelings or happiness. Sometimes we will need to say 'NO' to requests that we feel we cannot meet.

  One way of becoming clearer about whether you should agree to a request is to ask yourself, 'Am I doing this with a full heart?' If you can honestly answer 'Yes', then go ahead and do it. But if you answer 'No', then you are most likely doing it for the wrong reasons and this could lead to feelings of resentment that will ultimately erode the positive aspects of the relationship.

  It is OK to say 'No'. The other person *will* cope and in any case, their feelings are not your responsibility. Sometimes if we try to rescue people, we are actually disempowering them, diverting them away from their own life path and lessons, and this is not in their best interests. Sometimes allowing someone to make their own decisions and take their own actions, even if it may seem 'wrong' to us, is part of the richness of their learning and personal development and we have no right distracting them from it. Remember the Butterfly story.
- Practise self-care. Keep your energy jug topped up and always give from the overflow. In our busy lives as mothers/fathers, partners, workers, community members, we constantly pour our energy out. It is important that we keep our energy jug topped up, so that we can keep doing the things that we want to do for our families, workplaces and communities. We do that by taking time to look after ourselves in whatever way we find nurturing. It could be listening to music, meditating, spending some time in nature, shopping, having a bath. This is particularly important for Aboriginal Australians and others

from collectivist societies, who tend to put the needs of family or community members ahead of their own needs.

Self-care is NOT being selfish, it is essential in order to continue being a sustainable resource to others who matter to us. Instead of draining our energy jugs and becoming exhausted, lifeless or depressed, if we regularly top up, we are always giving to others from the overflow and never depleting ourselves.

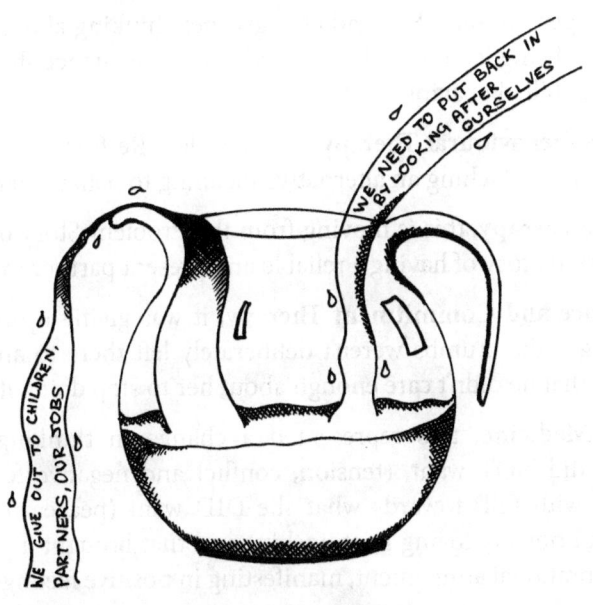

OUR ENERGY JUG

Just recently, I read a story from a woman who had been married for more than forty years to a man who routinely each morning woke before her, made toast for his breakfast every day, and left crumbs on the kitchen benchtop. When she awoke, she would see the crumbs and feel compelled to clean them up before she felt free to get her own breakfast. Over the years, she had raised this issue with her husband, but it had failed to cause any change in his behaviour.

It wasn't irritating him, but it had been irritating her for a long, long time and meant that she started each day of her married life agitated. Then, one morning as she walked into the kitchen and saw the crumbs on the bench as always, she had an epiphany. She suddenly thought 'What if I no longer had

Bill in my life? If Bill wasn't here any more, I would wake up and there would be no crumbs on the bench.'

This thought caused her such profound sadness that from that day on she looked at the crumbs on the bench in an entirely different light: she appreciated them being there, because it was evidence that she still had Bill, and all that he contributed to her life and she was grateful.

You can see from the above story, that nothing in the woman's external world had changed. She still had crumbs on the bench every morning, but she had changed her perception. She had changed her thinking about the *meaning* of the crumbs being left on the bench, and as a consequence she changed her feelings about Bill's behaviour.

In **Cognitive-behavioural Therapy**, this is called 'Re-framing' or 'Cognitive Re-structuring' - attaching an alternative meaning to behaviours or events.

In **Narrative Therapy**, this is moving from the Problem-Story of the crumbs to the Preferred Story of having a reliable and present partner in life.

In **Acceptance and Commitment Therapy**, it was giving up the resistance and defusing – the crumbs weren't deliberately left there to annoy her and didn't mean that he didn't care enough about her to stop doing it.

In **Energy Medicine**, this represented a change in thinking from what the woman did NOT want, (tension, conflict and negative feelings in her relationship with Bill) towards what she DID want (peace and acceptance in an unconditionally loving relationship) and that brought a consequential change in vibrational attunement, manifesting in positive feelings and energy.

Now she values seeing the crumbs each morning and starts her day with a full heart.

An Inventory of My Current Primary Relationships

How healthy are my personal relationships?

Do I have someone that I can talk to about the things that matter most to me?

How many people are there around me who I can trust to support me in times of need?

1.
2.
3.
4.
5.

Do I feel respected and valued in my relationships?

- With my spouse/partner
- With my children
- With my broader family
- With my work colleagues
- With my friends

Are there any relationships that violate my values or are toxic?

(Endnotes)
1. Putnam, Robert D. *Bowling Alone – the Collapse and Revival of American Community.* (USA: Touchstone Books, 2002.)

Chapter 13 – Nurture Your Soul

You have to grow from the inside out. None can teach you, none can make you spiritual. There is no other teacher but your own soul.

Swami Vivekananda

Our days are often busy and our minds constantly filled with what Buddhists call 'monkey chatter' – even more so now with access to the world wide web and social media. I often observe that young people especially seem to never not be doing something. Even when 'relaxing' at the end of the day, they are relentlessly texting on phones, or messaging on social media sites, or keying in to laptops or iPads. I find myself wondering if they ever experience silence or solitude.

As Mother Teresa said: 'We need to find God and he cannot be found in noise and restlessness. God is the friend of silence. See how nature – trees, flowers, grass – grow in silence; see the stars, the moon and the sun, how they move in silence…We need silence to be able to touch souls.'

Spirituality, Soulfulness. What do these things actually mean in today's secular society? I am no expert on all things spiritual. I am a student, but I think they mean being as fully you as you know how to be in the present. That is: knowing as much as you can about yourself; doing the things that you know bring pleasure to you and those around you; being engaged and connected; feeling alive and having a sense that life is good and more than what your biological senses can experience. An absence of negativity, pain or suffering is not necessary, nor is it necessary to have certain possessions or a certain level of wealth. Rather spirituality or soulfulness is a state of mind that is capable of transcending limitations and appreciating all that is, all that has gone before and all that is yet to come. It is about connection – to your 'higher' self, to others, to the entire universe. It is about 'wholeness' and 'authenticity'.

Now remember when I use words like 'soul', or 'spirituality' I am not necessarily referring to a god or to any specifically religious icon or idea (although if you do, that is perfectly fine).

Rather, I am referring to the notion of transcendence, the ability to move away from the mundane and ordinary, and connect with something larger than ourselves, in whatever way works for us.

Soulful connection is the ability to transcend the experience of the day to day routine, worries and concerns and connect to something more vast. Some people call this experience 'God', 'the Universe', 'my higher self', 'being in the zone' or 'being in flow'; Aboriginal people will talk about 'the Dreaming.' What you call it doesn't matter, it is the experience that is important. For those of you who have not been raised in any religious tradition, or have no current religious affiliation, you can define for yourself what your spirituality or soulfulness is and how to give expression to it.

There seems to be much evidence of loss of soul in today's Western world, and here in Australia it is evident across all age groups and ethnic groups, including Indigenous Australians. You only have to look at the high incidence of depression, anxiety and drug and alcohol addiction as evidence of disconnection. I often observe this lack of soul or spiritual connection most acutely in our Indigenous community, many of whom have lost connection to country and culture, either through historical government policy to force cultural disconnection, or through family breakdown and lack of continuity of narratives and lore.

Whilst writing this book I met and talked with Indigenous elders about the inter-generational impact of the dispossession of Indigenous Australians from their lands, the forcible removal of children and the dismantling of families, which resulted in individual members being dispersed far and wide, away from their traditional and custodial lands, from family members and other forms of identity and connection. These elders were expressing their concern about their young people being lost. When we understand the nature of the connection to land for Aboriginal people, we sense that this forced removal must have been personally and communally devastating.

Spiritual Connection to the Earth
David Tacey, Professor in Humanities and Social Sciences at La Trobe University, describes the Aboriginal connection to landscape and country this way: 'Landscape is at the centre of everything: at once the source of life, the origin of the tribe, the metamorphosed body of blood-line ancestors, and the intelligent force that drives the individual and creates society.'[1] There is no separation of 'self' from country, or from ancestors.

Spiritual healing, not more government handouts, seems imperative at this time in our history. It is encouraging to see Healing Centres now being funded and established around Australia to provide locally managed centres concerned with harnessing a range of healing resources. These include cultural knowledge and practices such as bush medicine, bush tucker, traditional tools, languages, men's and women's business, artwork, lore and custom, kinship systems, songlines and dreamtime stories, and spiritual wisdom. Connection or re-connection to country is an important part of the work of Healing Centres, encouraging Indigenous people to return to custodial lands to camp, yarn and practice culture with other community members – 'the mob'.

We have opportunities to learn from our Indigenous people – the oldest surviving culture in history – particularly those of us who came to this country as immigrants – who may have lost connection ourselves to land, ancestors and extended family, custom and tradition – and feel similarly displaced and disconnected.

As someone who was not raised with any religious tradition and is an immigrant from far away lands, I feel very privileged to have been given opportunities to learn about Australian Aboriginal spirituality, the importance of connection to country and ancestors who exist in timeless expression within features of the lands. I believe this spirituality has a lot to offer contemporary Australian society.

Indigenous spirituality has often been referred to, in English, as 'the Dreaming' or 'the Dreamtime'. This followed published conversations between Professor W. E. H. Stanner with Elders of the Arrernte in the early years of last century, when an attempt was made to describe 'tjukurpa' - the state between sleeping and wakefulness, where people connect to the spirit world.

> 'The Dreaming' or 'the Dreamtime' indicates a psychic state in which or during which contact is made with the ancestral spirits, or the Law, or that Special period of the beginning.'
>
> *Mudrooroo, Aboriginal Writer*

The *Dreaming* has never been a direct translation from an Aboriginal word. Indeed the English language does not have a word that is capable of capturing complex Aboriginal spiritual concepts such as 'tjurkurpa'. Aboriginal languages contain many words for spirituality and beliefs, the most well known of which seems to be *tjurkurrpa, jukurrpa, tjurgurba*, attributed in various sources to either the Pitjantjatjara or Arrernte people of north-western South Australia. Most Aboriginal writers on the subject suggest using 'Dreaming' rather than 'Dreamtime' because none of the hundreds of Aboriginal languages contain a word for *time*.

> 'We are the oldest and the strongest people, we're here all of the time, we're constant through the Dreaming which is happening now, there's no such thing as the Dreamtime.'
>
> *Karl Telfer, senior culture-bearer for Kaurna people, Adelaide.*

Most Aboriginal people show enormous generosity in welcoming non-Aboriginal interest in their history and their cultural and spiritual traditions. The late Bungal (David) Mowaljarlai, Ngarinyin activist, cultural recorder, storyteller, artist, and musician from the Northern Kimberley, in an interview on ABC Radio in 1995 said:

> *'What we see is, all the white people that were born in this country and they are missing the things that came from us mob, and we want to try and share it. And the people were born in this country, in this law country, from all these sacred places in the earth. And they were born on top of that.*
>
> *And that, we call wungud – very precious. That is where their spirit come from. That's why we can't divide one another, we want to share our gift, that everybody is belonging, we want to share together in the future for other generations to live on.'*

Where I live in south-west Victoria, the two local Aboriginal corporations are actively engaging with non-Indigenous Australians around cultural issues. One is involved in teaching cultural awareness to health professionals; the other is involved in a tourism venture designed to allow access to significant cultural sites, incorporating a former mission and geographical locations containing evidence of early traditional Gunditjmara settlements in an area known as Budj Bim.

> 'Tourism is a good way (to pass on cultural knowledge) and it helps to build pride in our young people and helps them to have confidence when talking with whitefellas.'
>
> *Dillon Andrews, Bungoolee Aboriginal Tours, Fitzroy Crossing, Western Australia.*

I am so grateful for the generosity of the Aboriginal people with whom I have worked – embracing and trusting me, sharing their information, stories and wisdom and showing enormous patience with my endless curiosity, since I have a great deal more to learn and understand. Although some aspects of culture are prohibited from sharing, most local Indigenous people genuinely take enormous pride in sharing aspects of their history and culture with non-Indigenous Australians and overseas visitors in the spirit of mutual respect and understanding.

I feel hopeful that we are at the start of a very exciting time in Australia where Indigenous and non-Indigenous Australians have the opportunity to heal together, as we acknowledge the injustices of the past and work to create a more tolerant, inclusive, compassionate, just and mutually respectful future. I believe that this could also lead us into what David Tacey has called 'A New Dreaming' – a new spirituality, with country at its centre.

Secular Spirituality

So, how do those of us with no religious tradition, begin to develop connection to a secular spirituality? Secular spirituality is defined in a way that is similar to the qualities of a spiritual life, which you may recall was outlined earlier in this book by the Dalai Lama:

> '*Secular spirituality emphasizes* humanistic *qualities such as love,* compassion, *patience, forgiveness, responsibility, harmony and a concern for others. Aspects of life and human experience which go beyond a purely materialist view of the world, without necessarily accepting belief in a supernatural reality or divine being. Spiritual practices such as mindfulness and meditation can be experienced as beneficial or even necessary for human fulfillment without any supernatural interpretation or explanation. Spirituality in this context may be a matter of nurturing thoughts, emotions, words and actions that are in harmony with a belief that everything in the universe is mutually dependent.*'

This non-theistic (not having a belief or involvement of a god or gods) approach to spirituality is also common to Indigenous spirituality, which sees spirit in 'everywhen' (a term coined by Stanner) – the past, the present, the future and incorporating relatedness between all living things, people, plants, animals and physical features of the land such as mountains, creeks and rocks.

In order to be open to spiritual experience, we need to open a space – we need to take a break from the noise, the busyness, the distractions. We need quiet time and space to go within, in order to have a chance of reaching this transcendent state and accessing the voice of our soul. It doesn't have to be in any particular place or setting, or take any particular amount of time. Soulfulness is a very personal matter – you just need time with yourself. It may be helpful though to be in an environment that is free of distraction, and which is sensorily pleasing to you. Interestingly, Aboriginal people are familiar with this need for silence:

> 'Dadirri: A special quality, a unique gift of the Aboriginal people, is inner deep listening and quiet still awareness. Dadirri recognises the deep spring that is inside us. It is something like what you call contemplation. The contemplative way of Dadirri spreads over our whole life. It renews us and brings us peace. It makes us feel whole again. In our Aboriginal way we learnt to listen from our earliest times. We could not live good and useful lives unless we listened. We are not threatened by silence. We are completely at home in it. Our Aboriginal way has taught us to be still and wait. We do not try to hurry things up. We let them follow their natural course – like the seasons.'
>
> *Miriam-Rose Ungunmerr-Baumann, cited in Grieves, V. Co-operative Research Centre for Aboriginal Health, Discussion Paper No 9 – Aboriginal Spirituality: Aboriginal Philosophy, 2009.*

It seems to me that connection to land in a spiritual sense has the capacity to bring Indigenous and non-Indigenous Australians together in environmental and conservation issues as well as spirituality – healing and protecting our earth. I am aware that elders within both Indigenous and non-Indigenous communities share concerns about the lack of values, lack of respect and connection for our young people with elders and traditions, and anxieties about the state of our earth, the pollution and degradation of our natural environment and its ability to sustain life into the future. These cultural and ecological shared concerns could become a catalyst in bringing all Australians together in a more spiritual relationship to the land we share, which would provide new depth and meaning to our lives and relationships with others.

David Tacey says: 'Politicians and media commentators sometimes pay lip service to the special relationship to the land that is integral to Aboriginal culture, but unless non-Aboriginals have experienced a psychic connection to landscape they will not learn to respect the mythic bond between this land and its indigenous inhabitants. Political goodwill alone will do very little to bridge the gap between cultures.

The same is true of our ecological crisis: we can urge each other to care more about the environment, but until we have revised our sense of identity to include the natural world, our best intentions may be in vain. The cure for our ecologically disastrous abuse of the earth and for our culturally debilitating racism is the spiritual renewal of consciousness.'

In sequels to *Care of the Soul* such as *The Re-enchantment of Everyday Life* and *The Soul's Religion*, Thomas Moore also invites his readers to consider finding soul in the natural world and culture, in the everyday world – in trees, food, home, garden, art, furniture, stories, and ritual, but acknowledges the difficulty for those of us in contemporary Western countries. 'Attending to nature is a spiritual exercise whether or not it goes by that name. It is a particular kind of contemplation. Not empty, except that the lens is not still. Not full, because there is no agenda.

It could be part of a spiritual practice, and indeed in some instances it is the major part. But this ritual asks for an attitude not congenial in a world given to action.'[2]

He advises us to pay attention to the environments in which we spend our time. Are they pleasing to your senses? Do you have a space that is welcoming with sensual fragrances, colours, textures? Is the place you work or live nurturing to your soul? How could you make it more so?

For me, the natural environment is important for my soul nurturance and I ensure that I schedule regular opportunities for spending time in the forest and on the beach. Sometimes I need not go anywhere, but just take notice of the wind in my hair and the warmth of the sun on my back.

Sometimes I just gaze out of the window at the sea, the grass, the trees, the birds and I am transformed and energised. I am lucky to live in a rural environment with lots of trees and wildlife and the sea in front of me. I find that stopping and taking in the view transports me away from the monkey chatter, the worries and concerns, the trivial, and re-energises me. I also find I need elements from the natural world within my home and place of work; so I am attracted to timber furniture. I like to have fresh flowers and fragrances around me, and I like natural, earthy colours and fabrics.

When I was a child, my parents would often bundle all six of us children into the station wagon to go for a picnic somewhere in the Adelaide Hills, or to a beach, or to a parkland. We would play 'I Spy with My Little Eye' – a game where we had to guess what an object was, starting with a particular letter of the alphabet, that was out in the landscape that we were driving through. We were regularly sent outside to play and at school, the day often started with a run around the oval. These days it saddens me to see babies parked in front of television sets, young children in cars with DVD players, whilst Mum and

Dad are texting, or – playing their own music – whilst the outside landscape just slips by unnoticed. Young people's recreational and leisure time no longer means being outdoors in nature with others. Rather it is too often linked to playing technological games, inside and alone, often simultaneously snacking on low-nutrient foods.

Engaging with nature, either in solitude or with others, offers considerable benefits for our physical, emotional and spiritual health. Any efforts to increase opportunities for engagement among our young people cannot help but lead to healthier, happier and more holistically healthy, rounded adults.

Can you identify what your passions are? Can you identify things that make your heart sing? Music, nature, art – even the simplest things in life can lead us into soul and spirit connection.

If you are having difficulty trying to find what it is that nurtures your soul it may be helpful to recall what you daydreamed about as a child, or the things that brought you pleasure and took you 'out of yourself'.

I have early memories of having the wind over my face. My mother tells me that she put each of her babies out in the fresh air in our prams and although I have no cognitive memory of this, as I was less than twelve months old, whenever I experience the sensation of the wind across my face, I feel transported. I feel safe, secure and warm, just like an infant wrapped up lovingly and securely in her pram. As a child I must have unconsciously attempted to recreate these feelings by laying in long grass on sunny days, feeling the breeze over my face.

To this day, I love to feel the wind in my face and have regular opportunities to experience that by walking on my property on top of a windy hill, or along the sandy beach nearby. The wind in my face seems to amalgamate all of those earlier experiences and I feel connection to something more. I feel the sum of my feelings from all of those earlier experiences.

I also used to draw a lot when I was a child, and although I don't do a great deal at present, I experience that sense of 'flow' when I do draw. I am taken away into the drawing and time just seems to pass without me noticing. Some people experience this when they are reading, listening to or playing music. The music I play often varies according to what I might be feeling emotionally – rock and roll if I feel exuberant, ballads if I feel more circumspect – but whatever the music, it transports me away from my daily routines and I ascend into a state of joyfulness. Music was also very much a part of my early family life too. Reconnecting to things of our childhood that gave us pleasure can offer a sense of connection and continuity, which can feel very comforting and nurturing whenever we experience them again in the present.

Make a commitment to allow yourself some quiet, reflective time alone. There, within the silence, listen carefully and you may just hear the voice of soul. It doesn't need to be any more than thirty minutes each day, but just be still, be present and be open.

For Indigenous Australians, this may involve going to country and listening for the voices of your ancestors, noticing the evidence of their former existence in the landscape, or through totem connection.

Once you identify the things that fill your heart and nourish your soul, make sure they are regularly accessible and present in your life.

The Importance of Ritual and Ceremony

Ritual and ceremony exist in most societies. They serve as a way of maintaining connection to past and ensuring continuity into the future.

Practices that were undertaken many years or generations ago continue to be practised today and we anticipate that they will be practised in years to come. This anticipation provides us with a continuum of connection from ancestors through to future generations. In the past, much of our ritual and ceremony came from religious practice such as confirmation, holy communion, marriage, baptism or christening – many of which evolved out of ancient pagan rituals, which were linked to the natural cycles of the earth, sun and moon. In today's more secular society, new traditions have emerged, including naming ceremonies rather than christenings and less formal wedding ceremonies in gardens and parks. Some groups have rituals or rites that mark developmental changes through life. When a child starts school for example, when they reach puberty, or when they graduate. Rituals and ceremonies provide increasingly rare opportunities for members of extended families to come together these days. From the very oldest to the very youngest, people gather together at weddings, christenings, or funerals.

If you are involved in a church you are likely to already be participating in its rituals and ceremonies.

If you are not, it is really open to you to decide what celebrations and rituals are important in providing that sense of nurturance, connection and continuity across members of family and community, and across time. They can include the simplest of daily or regular rituals. Having a cup of tea in a special tea cup for example, or in a special place; rubbing in a beautifully fragrant and moisturising hand-cream; drinking a glass of wine, or a non- alcoholic drink after dinner in a beautiful crystal glass whilst relaxing in your most comfortable armchair, soaking in a relaxing bubble bath on a Friday night at the end of your working week. Look for the things that feed or nourish your soul – including aesthetics – and try to incorporate them regularly into your daily living.

Soul can be found in the everyday practices and external environments of our lives, according to Thomas Moore in *The Re-Enchantment of Everyday Life*. He describes the way that the modern scientific and cerebral world has caused a disconnection from soul.

'The soul has an absolute, unforgiving need for regular excursions into enchantment. It requires them like the body needs food and the mind needs thought. Yet our culture often takes pride in disproving and exploding the sources of enchantment, explaining away one mystery after another and overturning precious shrines, dissolving the family farm that has housed spirits of civility for eons, or desecrating for material profit a mountain or stream sacred to native residents. We have yet to learn that we can't survive without enchantment and that the loss of it is killing us.'[3]

Writing in the mid-1990s when women were trying to have it and be it all – Sarah Ban Breathnach wrote a book called *Simple Abundance – A Daybook of Comfort and Joy*, in response to her own disenchantment with life. 'I couldn't remember the last time I was kind to myself. Was I ever? More often than it feels comfortable to admit, I was an angry, envious woman, constantly comparing myself to others only to become resentful because of what seemed to be missing from my life, although I couldn't have told you what it was.'[4] Her book evolved from her own re-evaluation of her life and unfolded into a form she could not have predicted when she started writing.

Like Thomas Moore, Sarah Breathnach encourages us to seek soul in the ordinary, everyday events of our lives. '*Simple Abundance* has enabled me to encounter everyday epiphanies, find the Sacred in the ordinary, the Mystical in the mundane, fully enter into the sacrament of the present moment.

I've made the unexpected but thrilling discovery that everything in my life is significant enough to be a continuous source of reflection, revelation, and reconnection: bad hair, mood swings, car pools, excruciating deadlines, overdrawn bank accounts, dirty floors, grocery shopping, exhaustion, illness, nothing to wear, unexpected company, even the final twenty-five pounds. *Simple Abundance* has reminded me what to do with a few loaves and fishes and has shown me how to spin straw into gold. *Simple Abundance* has given me the transcendent awareness that an authentic life is the most personal form of worship. Everyday life has become my prayer.'

Although a little frustrating to the Southern Hemisphere reader because the seasons are out of sync with our own, *Simple Abundance* is a great book for discovering your soulfulness, your authenticity, with readings for each day of the year.

Finally, soulfulness is not necessarily a serious business – it is about finding what feels good in your heart. Sometimes there is a great deal of soul nurturance in lightening up, being silly, in having fun, getting dirty, wet, covered in paint with your children or grand-children. See if you can find things that make you laugh and do them regularly – laughter is good for your physical, emotional and spiritual health.

Many of you have probably heard of the benefits of laughter therapy, or laughter yoga – the act of smiling and/or laughing, which provides bio-feedback from the muscles involved to the brain, which in turn releases endorphins, positive feel-good chemicals into the brain.

I heard of a study in which depressed patients were encouraged to smile for a period of time each day. The simple act of moving the muscles associated with smiling (whether the study participants actually felt happy or not) significantly reduced their symptoms of depression.

I am troubled by the large numbers of people, mostly women, who are having their smile lines removed from their faces with botox because it means the loss of that beneficial bio-feedback mechanism. If you really want to remove creases or wrinkles from your face, consider targeting the ones associated with negative emotion like your frown lines or the downturn at the side of your mouth!

In summary, some of us have either never had or have lost connection with our 'soul', with transcendence, with a sense of something bigger than ourselves – of connection to all that is and all that has gone before. We need to make time for solitude in order to hear the voice of our soul.

Remember to express gratitude for all that is right and good; remain connected to your authentic self and what you really want for your life; discover or rediscover your passions, the things that make your heart sing and you will experience the sacred in everyday life.

Ways to Enhance Your Soul Connection

- Make time for solitude – find some time regularly for quiet, stillness, reflection, contemplation

- Rediscover your passions – what used to take you 'outside yourself' when you were younger? What do you love to do now for the pure enjoyment of it?

- Spend time in the natural environment

- Consider making contact with local Aboriginal people to appreciate their spirituality and connection to land

- Listen to or play music

- Appreciate beauty – whether natural beauty in the environment, or through created works such as art, architecture, etc.

- Rediscover your inner child, be silly and have fun

- Learn to accept and appreciate everyday events as evidence of the fullness of your life

(Endnotes)
1. Tacey, David J. *Edge of the Sacred – Transformation in Australia*. (Aust: Harper-Collins, 1998).
2. Moore, Thomas. *The Soul's Religion – Cultivating a Profoundly Spiritual Way of Life*. (USA: HarperCollins, 2002).
3. Moore, Thomas. *The Re-enchantment of Everyday Life*. USA: Harper Collins, 1996.
4. Breathnach, Sarah Ban. *Simple Abundance – A Daybook of Comfort and Joy*. (Aust: Hodder & Stoughton, 1996).

Chapter 14 – Get Involved in Life

To have a purpose that is worthwhile, and that is steadily being accomplished, that is one of the secrets of a life that is worth living.

Herbert Casson (1869-1951)

The world's happiest people are active people, engaged in meaningful activities and relationships and feeling a sense of accomplishment from having achieved personal goals. So, in what ways could you be involved in things that:

- Inspire you
- Give meaning to your life
- Ignite your passions
- Give expression to your identified values
- Help you to make a difference
- Allow you to give expression to your unique talents, skills and attributes?

Richard Schoch says: 'Action is the heart of an authentically happy existence, because only in action do we attain fulfilment….. Through purposeful action, you become your future and in it find your contentment…..To search for happiness is not to embark on a voyage to a distant exotic land, but to return home.'[1]

In the opening chapter of this book, I talked about how I believe some of us feel disempowered and so have handed over much of the decision-making of our lives to others who do not know us. We have become disempowered within the medical system, our food production system, our political systems and as a result of the increasing professionalization of our lives. Some of us have lost our confidence and become reliant on so-called, self-professed 'experts' to advise us on how to live our lives across all domains: health, relationships, employment, finances, leisure-time.

I hope that at this stage of your reading, and through the exercises in previous chapters, you have begun to know yourself and reconnect to your inherent strengths and competencies in such a way that you now feel greater confidence in your own ability to manage all aspects of your own life.

I have shown that as social beings, our happiness is intimately linked to others and yet research suggests that our social capital (our shared values and norms and involvement in our political and social institutions) is declining, with fewer people actively engaging in serving on committees, attending public meetings, or being involved with political parties. One researcher, Robert D. Putnam, cites the reasons for this as including the increasing participation of women in the workforce and the increasing 'individualisation' of our recreational activities (watching television, computer games and the internet). He notes in his book *Bowling Alone: The Collapse and Revival of American Community*, that although the number of people who bowl in the United States has increased, the number of people who bowl in leagues, or teams has decreased. When people bowl alone, they do not participate in social interaction and the kinds of civic discussions that might have occurred whilst bowling with others in a team environment. Referred to as 'social capital decline', Putnam has urged governments to undertake studies to highlight which forms of associations can create the greatest social capital and how it may be influenced by technology, social equality and public policy, in order to reverse the recent trend of declining social capital.[2]

In this technological age we have access to more information than we have at any other time before and we have the ability to connect with thousands, even millions of others around the globe in order to actively contribute to changing the world in whatever small (or large) way is important to us.

Whether you are an introvert or extrovert there are now ways in which you can have your say and make a difference. It is time to get informed, get together and get active!

This is what changes the world – but remember to be *for* things rather than *against* and be focussed on what you *do want* rather than what you *don't want* – so be for honesty and ethics in medicine and food production, rather than against the increasing domination of pharmaceutical companies or against genetic modification, for example.

> Never believe that a few caring people can't change the world. For, indeed, it is the only thing that ever has.
>
> *Margaret Mead*

Many of us have become discouraged with the lack of moral or ethical leadership in our countries of the western world, many experiencing an increasing gulf between public and private standards, which leaves us feeling uncertain and unsafe and has led to us withdrawing from social and political activity. Richard Eckersley notes: 'Societies usually try to maintain a public standard of ethics that is higher than the private, so as to set an example, so as to inspire people to try harder. Yet today the reverse is true. This produces a growing sense of alienation and disengagement from social institutions, a deepening cynicism that excuses us from doing anything about behaviour – ours or others' – that we know to be wrong.'[3]

I think, and I hope, that the days of political apathy and inactivity and social disengagement are coming to an end, now that so many key issues relating to our health, the health of our children and our planet has reached critical mass and can no longer be overlooked.

> 'If, for any reason whatsoever, moral standards are conspicuously and unprecedentedly breached in one area of society, such as the political, it will follow as the night the day that those standards will start collapsing all down the line – in sports, entertainment, education, the armed forces, business and government.'
>
> Margaret Halsey (1910 – 1997)

There are new ways for us – whether extrovert or introvert – to be actively involved in expressing our opinions in relation to the decisions that our governments make. In Australia, for example, the group *GetUp* is a great example of an on-line social action group that allows involvement for many ordinary citizens at whatever level they may feel comfortable – pledging support on a particular issue, donating time or money, writing letters to politicians, attending events, are all examples of ways in which you can find your voice and have it heard. *GetUp* is an independent, grass-roots community organisation, which aims to provide everyday Australians with the opportunity to participate in our democracy and it seeks to hold politicians accountable on important issues.

GetUp is non-party political and 'aims to build an accountable and progressive Australia – an Australia which values economic fairness, social justice and environmental sustainability at its core.'[4] Currently for example, *GetUp* is campaigning around protecting the Great Barrier Reef and changing Australia's treatment of asylum-seekers.

Alternatively, *Change.org* is a global petition platform that collects support for issues that can be local, national, or global in character and bring pressure to bear on governments or corporations to implement the change being requested. Their website says:

'There are more than 45 million *Change.org* users in 196 countries, and every day people use our tools to transform their communities – locally, nationally and globally. Whether it's a mother fighting bullying in her daughter's school, customers pressing banks to drop unfair fees, or citizens holding corrupt officials to account, thousands of campaigns started by people like you have won on *Change.org* – and more are winning every week.'

Many younger people are using social network sites to set up issues-based pages to gather and mobilise popular support in response to decisions of government or multi-national corporations with which they disagree or feel negatively impacted by.

There have been many examples of governments either delaying or reversing controversial policy decisions as a consequence of the expression and publication of such large, mass counter-views.

> I slept and dreamed that life was joy,
>
> I awoke and saw that life was duty,
>
> I acted, and behold: duty was joy.
>
> *Rabindranath Tagore (1861-1941)*

There is increasing public concern, I believe, in relation to the blurring of boundaries between health science and economics, specifically when seemingly 'evidence-based' research is shaped by market considerations, rather than what is in the best interests of the consumer together with the increasing merging of the interests of big business, government and medicine.

As Margaret Mead says, don't underestimate the power of your voice, particularly when it is joined together with others. We have become sidelined and silenced in the political processes of our countries in recent years, but it is time to step-up, and say what we think and believe in. We have identified values that give our lives meaning and we want those values to be reflected in the actions of our governments and businesses. Many feel we can no longer trust our leaders to do what is right, to do what is ethical, to do what is in the best interests of their citizens and this has led us to withdraw from the processes from which we feel alienated. 'Increasingly, our leaders, public and private, are *at best* [my emphasis] doing what is legal, not what is ethical.'[5] The continuing drive by governments and the corporate sector for more economic growth, most of which is achieved through rampant consumerism, is becoming increasingly out of step with the general community who have seen the excesses of consumerism. The increasing levels of alienation and demoralisation is evident in the escalating levels of depression, anxiety, drug-taking and chronic disease and more and more people are desperately searching for a new world view that is more compassionate, more collectivist, more ecologically sustainable, more ethical and spiritual.

American psychologist, Tim Kasser has researched the effects of materialist values including the pursuit of money and possessions on our wellbeing and found that rather than leading to increased levels of life satisfaction, a focus on materialism actually leads to increased dissatisfaction with life and can lead to depression, anxiety, anger and isolation. Human needs for security and safety, competence and self-esteem, connectedness to others, and autonomy and authenticity are relatively unsatisfied when materialistic values predominate, he says. [6]

Studies by a number of Australian psychologists have supported these findings, as have studies across several European countries that indicate that there is a comprehensive shift of values and worldview underway, and this research was conducted *prior to* the Global Financial Crisis: 'They are disenchanted with "owning more stuff", materialism, greed, me-firstism, status display, glaring social inequalities of race and class, society's failure to care adequately for elders, women and children, and the hedonism and cynicism that pass for realism in modern society. Instead, they are placing emphasis in their lives on relationships, communities, spirituality, nature and the environment, and real ecological sustainability.'[7] These are the things that will provide meaning and purpose in our lives and reduce the unprecedented levels of distress and existential emptiness caused by the combined impact of materialism and individualism.

Although withdrawal from a culturally hostile world may be an effective short-term strategy in actually protecting our emotional wellbeing, we can no longer afford to be disengaged from the social and political processes, which show no signs of being able to responsibly and ethically self-regulate.

In the interests of our children and future generations, we need to take back our political power, in order that events such as the global financial crisis, the disparity between celebrity and CEO incomes and the poor, the deliberate fraudulent manipulation of scientific research for economic profit, the poisoning of our food supply and the dishonesty within our medical system cannot keep occurring.

We can no longer allow our inactivity and silence to be misconstrued as amounting to our passive agreement and we cannot wait to be invited to express our truth. It is my belief from conversations with many others that:-

- We *do* want healthy, nutritious, chemical-free food
- We *do* want healthy, pollution free air to breathe
- We *do* want safe, healthy water to drink
- We *do* want our children to have the best chance to live long and healthy lives and not to suffer life-limiting, debilitating chronic illnesses
- We *do* want natural approaches to ending chronic disease where the evidence supports this
- We *do* want rigorous, independent, medical research free from manipulation by those with vested interests.
- We *do* want governments who place the health and welfare of its citizens above the profits of corporations.
- We *do* want wellbeing to be measured by more than economic values
- We *do* want a safe and honest medical system
- We *do* want sustainable practices and policies that ensure the ongoing viability of the earth and the human and non-human life it sustains

It is time for us to lobby for change in the health industry, to have it focus on wellness rather than illness, and put greater emphasis on the role of nutritional and environmental factors that contribute to good health rather than the increasing use of medications. It is time for us to step up and provide the ethical and moral leadership, which is not being universally provided by our civic and religious leaders.

> *'If, over the next decade, a critical mass of people with new priorities were to emerge, and if these people were seen to do well, in every sense of the term – if their co-operation with each other brings reciprocal benefits, if they find joy and contentment in their lives – then the ethical attitude will spread, and the conflict between ethics and self-interest will be shown to have been overcome, not by abstract reasoning alone, but by adopting the ethical life as a practical way of living, and showing that it works psychologically, socially and ecologically.'*[8]

The current world view with its individualistic, consumerist, economistic values are not working psychologically, socially or ecologically. Each of us must take the time to reflect on our own values and priorities. It is time to harness the growing voices of discontent and demand that our governments and corporations reflect our community values and concerns.

It is my firm conviction that a life lived well, with access to healthy, nutritious foods grown in healthy soils; positive, supportive relationships with self, others and community; an integrative, holistic health and medical system, values-based, ethical living supported and reflected by governments and corporations, and some form of spiritual connection and expression, whether religious or secular; may well be the antidote to the current high levels of depression, anxiety, alienation and chronic illness.

> It's the action,
>
> Not the fruit of the action,
>
> That's important.
>
> You have to do the right thing. It may not be in your power,
>
> May not be in your time,
>
> That there'll be any fruit.
>
> But that doesn't mean
>
> You stop doing the right thing.
>
> You may never know what results
>
> From your action.
>
> But if you do nothing,
>
> There will be no result.
>
> *Mahatma Gandhi (1869 – 1948)*

(Endnotes)

1. Schoch, Richard. *The Secrets of Happiness – Three Thousand Years of Searching For The Good Life*. (USA: Scribner, 2006).
2. Putnam, Robert D. *Bowling Alone: The Collapse and Revival of American Community*. (New York: Simon & Schuster, 2000).
3. Eckersley, Richard. *Well and Good – How We Feel and Why It Matters*. (Aust: Text Publishing, 2004).
4. http://www.getup.com.au
5. Eckersley, Richard. *Well and Good – How We Feel and Why It Matters*. (Aust: Text Publishing, 2004).
6. Kasser, Tim. "The High Price of Materialism", cited in Eckersley, Richard. *Well and Good – How We Feel and Why It Matters*. (Aust: Text Publishing, 2004).
7. Eckersley, Richard. *Well and Good – How We Feel and Why It Matters*. (Aust: Text Publishing, 2004).
8. Singer, Peter. *How Are We To Live – Ethics In An Age of Self-Interest*. (Aust: Random House, 1997).

Epilogue

You may now have deduced that the woman in the forest at the very start of the book was me. At the time I was suffering from clinical depression and sickening anxiety following the breakdown of my marriage and struggling with financial challenges and an uncertain future. My life has changed considerably since then and I now feel happy and fulfilled most of the time. The single biggest change I made to the way I lived was to stop focussing my attention on my problems, and start thinking about what I really wanted instead. That shift in thinking caused a radical shift in my experiences.

I share my stories in the hope of inspiring you to believe that you too can recover from depression and anxiety and take charge of your life. You *are* in control of your own thoughts. You *can* harness that power to create sustainable happiness.

Stay focussed on what you DO want.

Wishing you good health, happiness and a life of meaning, purpose and connection to others.

List of Illustrations

1. "Comfort" - Annette Taylor
2. Two ways up a mountain – Nigel Cooper
3. Meridian Points – Tony Ashby, Tony Ashby Art
4. The Energy Jug – Tony Ashby, Tony Ashby Art
5. The Communication Process – Howells, T.
6. Spheres or Bubbles of Perception – Howells, T.

Graphs and Tables

1. Changes in Rates of Selected Reported Chronic Diseases 1980-1994. USDC, 1996; Werbach, 1993; Nutrition Security Institute.
2. Minerals Go Down, Disease Goes Up - Nutrition Security Institute
3. Life Satisaction for Various Groups – Diener and Seligman, 2004.
4. Scale of Emotions – Ask and It is Given, Esther and Jerry Hicks
5. Eighty Year Decline in Mineral Content of One Medium Apple – Nutrition Security Institute
6. Nutrient Loss From Refining of Wheat – Schroeder, Henry R. American Journal of Clinical Nutrition, 1971.
7. Rates of Autism – Whiteout Press, http://worldtruth.tv/courts-quietly-confirm-mmr-vaccine-causes-autism, 20/09/13.
8. Deaths Per Year – Starfield, Barbara. John Hopkins School of Hygiene and Public Health
9. Societal vs Individual Risk of Death in Australia – Ron Law, Risk and Policy Adviser, Juderon Associates
10. World's Healthiest Foods rich in omega-3 fats – www.whfoods.org
11. Top Mood-boosting Foods – Howells, T.
12. Summary of Differences Between Time Out and Silent Treatment – www.outofthefog.net

Recommended Reading and Sources

> For information about Tess' workshops, schedule, books and products:
>
> www.tesshowells.com.au
>
> www.facebook.com/tesshowellspsychologist

Australian Aboriginal Culture

Burnum Burnum. *Aboriginal Australia – A Traveller's Guide*. Aust: Angus & Robertson, 1988.

Co-operative Research Centre for Aboriginal Health. http://www.crah.org.au

The Gunditjmara People with Gib Wettenhall. *The People of Budj Bim – Engineers of Aquaculture, Builders of Stone House Settlements and Warriors Defending Country*. Aust: Em Press Publishing, 2010.

Purdie, N., Dudgeon, P., Walker, R. *Working Together: Aboriginal and Torres Strait Islander Mental Health and Wellbeing Principles and Practice*. Aust: Commonwealth Government of Australia, 2010.

Reynolds, Henry. *Aborigines and Settlers – The Australian Experience 1788 – 1939*. Aust: Cassell, 1972.

SBS *First Australians – The Untold Story of Australia*. Aust: Blackfella Films/ First Nation Films, SBS Corpn., Screen Australia, NSW Film & Television Office, South Australian Film Corp., Screenwest, 2008.

Acceptance and Commitment Therapy (ACT)

Harris, Russ. *The Happiness Trap – How to Stop Struggling and Start Living*. USA: Trumpeter, 2008.

Affirmations

Hay, Louise. *You Can Heal Your Life*. Aust: Specialist Publications, 1988.

See also Law of Attraction

The Brain/Neuroscience

Goleman, Daniel. *Social Intelligence*. USA: Bantam Books, 2006.

Goleman, Daniel. *Destructive Emotions and How We Can Overcome Them*. A dialogue with the Dalai Lama. USA: Bantam Books, 2004.

Iacoboni, Marco. *Mirroring People – The Science of Empathy and How We Connect With Others*. USA: Picador, 2008.

Buddhism

Dalai Lama. *The Universe In a Single Atom – The Convergence of Science and Spirituality*. USA: Morgan Road Books, 2005.

Dalai Lama. *The Transformed Mind – Reflections on Truth, Love and Happiness*. UK: Hodder & Stoughton, 2000.

Cognitive-behavioural Therapy

Edelman, Sarah. *Change Your Thinking – Overcome Stress, Anxiety & Depression, and Improve Your Life with CBT*. New York: Marlowe & Co., 2007.

Wehrenberg, Margaret. The 10 Best Ever Depression Management Techniques. New York: W. W. Norton & Co., 2010.

Communication Skills

Bolton, Robert. People Skills, How to assert yourself, listen to others, and resolve conflicts. Prentice-Hill, USA, 1979.

Cornelius, H & Faire, S. *Everyone Can Win – How To Resolve Conflict*. Simon & Schuster, Aust. 1989.

Complementary/Integrative Medicine & Nutrition

Davis, William. *Wheat Belly – Lose the Wheat, Lose the Weight, and Find Your Path Back to Health*. USA: Rodale, 2011.

Jamison, Jennifer. *Clinical Guide to Nutrition and Dietary Supplements in Disease Management*. Aust: Churchill Livingstone, 2003.

Nutrition Security Institute: www.nutritionsecurity.org

Pollan, Michael. *In Defense of Food: An Eater's Manifesto*. USA: Gale, Cengage Learning, 2009.

Whitney, E. & Rolfes, S. R. *Understanding Nutrition – 13th Edition*. USA: Wadsworth, Cengage Learning, 2013.

Worlds' Healthiest Foods: www.whfoods.org

Depression/Anxiety & Recovery

Edelman, Sarah. *Change Your Thinking – Overcome Stress, Anxiety & Depression, and Improve Your Life with CBT*. New York: Marlowe & Co., 2007.

Howells, T. Daytime Relaxation CD or MP3

Howells, T. Night-time Relaxation CD or MP3

Moore, Thomas. *Dark Nights of the Soul – A Guide to Finding Your Way Through Life's Ordeals*. Piatkus, UK, 2004.

Moore, Thomas. *The Soul's Religion – Cultivating a Profoundly Spiritual Way of Life*. New York: Harper Perennial, 2003.

Wehrenberg, Margaret. *The 10 Best Ever Depression Management Techniques*. New York: W. W. Norton & Co., 2010.

Emotional Freedom Technique, Thought Field Therapy (TFT) and Tapping

Callahan, Roger J. *Tapping the Healer Within – Using Thought Field Therapy to Instantly Conquer Your Fears, Anxieties, and Emotional Distress*. USA: McGraw-Hill, 2001.

Ortner, Nick. *The Tapping Solution – A Revolutionary System for Stress-Free Living*. UK: Hay House, 2011.

Ethics

Dalai Lama. *Ethics for the New Millennium*. USA: Riverhead Books, 1999.

Eckersley, Richard. *Well and Good – How We Feel and Why it Matters*. Aust: Text Publishing, 2004.

Mackay, H. *Right and Wrong – How to decide for yourself*. Aust: Hodder, 2004.

Singer, Peter. *How Are We To Live – Ethics In An Age of Self-Interest*. Aust: Random House, 1997.

Happiness

Ben-Shahar, Tal. *Happier – Learn the Secrets to Daily Joy and Lasting Fulfilment*. USA: McGraw-Hill, 2007.

Csikszentmihalyi, Mihaly. *Flow – The Psychology of Optimal Experience*. New York: Harper Perennial, 2008.

The Dalai Lama. *Happiness in a Material World*. Aust: Lothian Books, 2002

The Dalai Lama & Cutler, H.C. *The Art of Happiness – A Handbook for Living*. Aust: Hodder, 1998.

Diener, Ed and Biswas-Diener, Robert. *Happiness – Unlocking the Mysteries of Psychological Wealth*. USA: Blackwell Publishing, 2008.

Klein, Stefan. *The Science of Happiness – How Our Brains Make Us Happy – and What We Can Do to Get Happier*. Aust: Scribe, 2006.

Layard, Richard. *Happiness – Lessons From a New Science*. UK: Penguin, 2005.

Ricard, Matthieu. *Happiness – A Guide to Developing Life's Most Important Skill*. UK: Atlantic Books, 2007.

Schoch, Richard. *The Secrets of Happiness – Three Thousand Years of Searching For the Good Life*. USA: Scribner, 2006.

Seligman, Martin E.P. *Authentic Happiness – Using the New Positive Psychology to realize Your Potential for Lasting Fulfillment.* Aust: Random House, 2002.

Seligman, Martin. *Flourish – A Visionary New Understanding of Happiness and Well-being.* Aust: Random House, 2011.

Health/Wellness/Nutrition

Day, Phillip. *Health Wars.* UK: Credence Publications, 2001.

Day, Phillip. *The Mind Game.* UK: Credence Publications, 2002.

Day, Phillip. *Food for Thought.* UK: Credence Publications, 2001.

Eckersley, Richard. *Well and Good – How We Feel and Why it Matters.* Aust: Text Publishing, 2004.

Introversion

Helgoe, Laurie. *Introvert Power – Why Your Inner Life is Your Hidden Strength.* USA: Sourcebooks Inc. 2008.

Laney, Marti Olsen. *The Introvert Advantage – How to Thrive in an Extrovert World.* USA: Workman Publishing, 2002.

Wagele, Elizabeth. *The Happy Introvert – A Wild and Crazy Guide for Celebrating Your True Self.* USA: Ulysses Press, 2006.

Law of Attraction

Hicks, Esther and Jerry. *Ask and It Is Given – Learning to Manifest Your Desires.* Aust: Hay House, 2004.

Hicks, Esther and Jerry. *The Law of Attraction – The Basics of the Teachings of Abraham.* USA: Hay House, 2006.

Hicks, Esther and Jerry. *The Amazing Power of Deliberate Intent – Living the Art of Allowing.* Hay House, 2006.

Hicks, Esther and Jerry. *The Astonishing Power of Emotions – Let Your Feelings Be Your Guide.* USA: Hay House, 2007.

Hicks, Esther and Jerry. *Money, and the Law of Attraction – Learning to Attract Wealth, Health, and Happiness.* Aust: Hay House, 2008.

Meditation and Mindfulness

Anderson, Michael. *Mindfulness Practice.* Aust: Australian Institute of Emotional Intelligence, 2004.

Harris, Russ. *The Happiness Trap – How to Stop Struggling and Start Living.* USA: Trumpeter, 2008.

Howells, T. Daytime Relaxation CD or MP3

Howells, T. Night-time Relaxation CD or MP3

Kabat-Zinn, John. *Wherever You Go There You Are – Mindfulness Meditation in Everyday Life.* New York: Hyperion, 2005.

Narrative Therapy

Morgan, Alice. *What is Narrative Therapy? An Easy-to-read introduction.* Aust: Dulwich Centre Publications, 2000.

White, Michael. *Reauthoring Lives: Interviews and Essays.* Aust: Dulwich Centre Publications, 1995.

Personality-based Job Selection

Tiegger, P. D. & Barron, B. *Do What You Are – Discover the Perfect Career for You Through the Secrets of Personality Type.* USA: Little, Brown & Co., 2007.

Philosophy/Psychology

de Botton, Alain. *The Consolations of Philosophy.* Aust: Penguin, 2000.

Frankl, Viktor E. *Man's Search For Meaning.* USA: Washington Square Press, 1984.

Kalat, James W. Biological Psychology, Tenth Edition. USA: Wadsworth, Cengage Learning, 2009.

Relationships

Chapman, G. *The Five Love Languages – How to Express Heartfelt Commitment to Your Mate.* USA: Northfield Publishing, 2005.

Fisher, Bruce. *Rebuilding When Your Relationship Ends.* USA: Impact Publishers, 1992.

Gottman, John M. *The Seven Principles for Making Marriage Work.* USA: Three Rivers Press, 1999.

Gottman, John M. *The Relationship Cure – A 5 Step Guide to Strengthening Your Marriage, Family and Friendships.* USA: Three Rivers Press, 2001.

Hendrix, Harville. *Getting the Love You Want – A Guide for Couples.* UK: Pocket Books, 2005.

Jansen, J. & Newman, M. *Really Relating – How to Build an Enduring Relationship.* Aust: Random House, 1989.

Montgomery, Bob & Evans, Lynette. *Living and Loving Together – A Practical step-by-step Manual to Help you Make and Keep Better Relationships.* Aust: Nelson, 1993.

Soulfulness/Spirituality

Breathnach, Sarah Ban. *Simple Abundance – A Daybook of Comfort and Joy.* Aust: Hodder & Stoughton, 1996.

Breathnach, Sarah Ban. *Something More – Excavating Your Authentic Self.* Aust: Hodder & Stoughton, 1998.

Dalai Lama. *The Universe In a Single Atom – The Convergence of Science and Spirituality.* USA: Morgan Road Books, 2005.

Emoto, Masaru. *The Secret Life of Water.* UK: Simon & Schuster, 2006.

Moore, Thomas. *Care of the Soul.* USA: Harper Collins, 1992.

Moore, Thomas. *The Re-Enchantment of Everyday Life.* USA: Harper Collins, 1996.

Moore, Thomas. *Dark Nights of the Soul – A Guide to Finding Your Way Through Life's Ordeals.* UK: Piatkus, 2004.

Moore, Thomas. *The Soul's Religion – Cultivating a Profoundly Spiritual Way of Life.* USA: Perennial, 2002.

Tacey, David J. *Edge of the Sacred – Transformation in Australia.* Aust: Harper Collins, 1998.

www.ingramcontent.com/pod-product-compliance
Lightning Source LLC
Chambersburg PA
CBHW050633160426
43194CB00010B/1649